Editors: Lawrence Ferlinghetti
                Nancy J. Peters

Staff Editors: Robert Sharrard
                Amy Scholder

Design: Patricia Fujii

Typesetting: Miller Freeman Publications

CITY LIGHTS
REVIEW

Number 2

City Lights Books
San Francisco

©1988 by City Lights Books
All Rights Reserved

Front cover: *Nocturne* by K. H. Hödicke, 1983
Illustrations for "Reminiscences," courtesy Jonas Mekas
"Letter from Goose Creek: April" by Marilyn Hacker first appeared in
Yellow Silk Journal
"The Death of the Resistance Fighter" by Ferdinando Camon is from
La Malattia Chiamata Uomo (Garzanti Editore, Milano).

The Library of Congress has catalogued this serial publication as follows:
  City Lights review. —No. 1- —San Francisco: City Lights Books, ©1987-

     v.:ill; 23 cm.

     1. Literature, Modern—20th century—Periodicals.

PN6010.5.C58   081—dcl9   87-640490
                                     AACR2 MARC-S
Library of Congress   ]8803]

City Lights Books are available to bookstores through our primary
distributor: Subterranean Company, P.O. Box 10233, Eugene, OR 97440.
[503] 343-6324. Our books are also available through library jobbers and
regional distributors. For personal orders and catalogs, please write to
City Lights Books, 261 Columbus Avenue, San Francisco CA 94133.

CITY LIGHTS BOOKS are edited by Lawrence Ferlinghetti and Nancy J.
Peters and published at the City Lights Bookstore, 261 Columbus
Avenue, San Francisco CA 94133.

CONTENTS

When Were the Sixties?
Where Are We Now?
A Meditation

TODD GITLIN

1

How shall we imagine the Sixties? Sequel or prologue? End or beginning? As one segment of a historical curve? Is it a rising or a falling curve? Or do the Sixties stand as a crazy spike in history? Were the Sixties the end of the Cold War liberal years? The prologue to the Reagan years? The destruction of the West, the beginning of the salvation of the West? Or a last gasp for the Enlightenment's revolutionary project, one of those amazing and infrequent moments in the history of the West (1789, 1848, 1917, 1968) when, across national boundaries, revolutionaries stormed heaven, assaulting the autocrats, swelling with apocalyptic desires to make humanity whole?

All of the above. Amazingly, history continues.

2

Myth is blocky and abstract, history is tangled and dense. Myth likes to soar, history is content to walk. Myth gives quick answers, history answers a question with two more questions. But there is nothing wrong, and a great deal right, with the quest for a usable myth—that is, a general notion. General notions have their use as long as they don't harden into grand theories riding roughshod over complexity.

Twenty years after the fact, popular culture force-feeds us on legends of the *annus mirabilis* 1968, the culminating moment in the whole heaven and hell of the Sixties. You can take your pick of two legendary versions: (A) the Sixties as glory days when millions of heroic flower children built barricades (or something) for peace or revolution (or something); (B) the Sixties as the witching hour when drug-crazed beasts desecrated the Great Books. In either version, the Sixties loom larger than life—safely so. The heroes and monsters have been scooped out of their historical moment. As icons, they have all the practical meaning of the endless golden-oldie commercials now pandering to those luscious baby-boom demographics on TV. Once extricated from the texture of real life— the product of real choices made by real humans in real situations— those ancient giants acquire all the majesty, or the cautionary power, of the dead.

But it is too easy to be too cynical about the ways of the media trend industry. The media exploit, they don't invent. The power of Sixties images to move us is something to take seriously; it can't be shrugged off as salesmanship pure and simple. Those images—students against bayonets, flowers in gun barrels, masses filling the boulevards, Martin Luther King going to the mountain, crowds tearing at Robert Kennedy—those images have the power to move eighteen-year-olds who are looking for a way to express something barely expressible today. To them, the legendary Sixties were a time when heroism was possible and public virtue had a place. Many of today's college students have jumped onto the treadmill to medical school, law school, or business school, but most of them seem to know there ought to be something else in life. They are not simply greedy or conformist, they are anxious about finding a place on the treadmill. They don't know whether they'll be able to afford to live in a place half the size of the one they grew up in. They're fascinated with a time when people picked their lives up in their hands

and tested limits—whether in personal experimentation or political action.

In many ways these images are daunting. Events of glorious or cataclysmic magnitude—accompanied by the purity of Joan Baez, the spleen of Bob Dylan, the anguish of Janis Joplin—seem to have taken place on another planet. No wonder young activists today feel burdened as much as inspired by the versions of the Sixties that descend to them. The sense of inspiration is real. But larger-than-life legends can be crushing.

3

What did the movements of the Sixties accomplish? The bitter Right answers: everything. In the Book of Revelations whose verses are being written alternately by George Will and Norman Podhoretz, the movements undermined legitimate authority and sapped the nation's vital fluids. They weakened the country's will to resist Communism. They took over the media and the universities, the national spawning grounds of ideology. They drove women out of the kitchen and criminals out of the jails. Having sung hymns to freedom, they ushered in sodomy and AIDS. Having rioted for peace, they softened the ground for a Reagan who, when he consults his index cards for "talking points," finds them filled with phrases of praise for Gorbachev.

Outside the Right, the question of what the movements of the Sixties accomplished is far harder to answer. My feelings are mixed. On the affirmative hand, significant shifts in popular sentiment and, to some extent, government policy:

• Blacks and women have made gains in political citizenship which, however contested, are unlikely to be rolled back. The black vote has become a major factor in Southern politics and, thanks to Jesse Jackson, the Democratic Party nationwide. Blacks and Hispanics play a large part in local governments.

• The right to choose abortion has been eroded but remains in force. Two Reagan administrations have failed to destroy reproductive rights—undermined and weakened them, yes, but not destroyed them. The principle of a woman's right to control her body has led to a strengthening of antirape consciousness and an increased understanding that the battering of women is a political issue. Some or another version of child care has become a consensual position among leading politicians. Despite rollbacks in popular culture, most American women consider themselves feminists.

• Activism has become normal. While voting declines and the power of money in politics grows, agitation spreads—on a host of issues, in a host of places, from a host of vantage points and class positions, and, of course, with mixed results. In other words, representative democracy has declined while at the same time there is a surge toward direct participation. Popular movements mushroom. Black students organize against upsurges of overt racism, while at the same time, inner city residents, unimpressed by the Rea-

gans' "just say no" campaign, demonstrate against the crack business. Meanwhile, a national student conference at Rutgers University in February drew 800 left activists. In March, demonstrations against the shipment of American troops to Honduras flashed up overnight in Chicago, Minneapolis, Boston, San Francisco, and other cities, involving tens of thousands. In April, the largest civil disobedience action in American history (over 2,000 people) took place—unnoticed by major media—at the Nevada nuclear test site. As I write, the energies focused and released by Jesse Jackson's campaign are formidable.

• Environmental consciousness has become normal. Public opinion wants to "preserve the environment" even when it costs money. (Government policy under Reagan is, of course, something else.) Even establishment institutions like the World Bank recognize the fragility of the world ecosystem.

• Anti-interventionism has become the modal position in America's international politics. Not mostly as a matter of principle; no, what the military and some of the top civilian leaders concluded from Vietnam is that wars ought to be fought by Third World proxies ("low intensity conflict") unless they are weekend wars, easily winnable and guaranteed popular. True, they have gotten away with a great deal of murder and mayhem. But the interventionists have a tremendous problem. Antiwar sentiment (medicalized into "the Vietnam syndrome") is strong enough that when Reagan, Casey and the rest of the Manifest Destinarians set out to carry on with interventionism as usual, to overthrow the Sandinistas, they had to set up a secret government apparatus to do it. To do so, they had to violate laws. They therefore fell afoul of the Constitution and the Congress. Congress, after hemming and hawing, tired of the contras in Nicaragua. All the 1988 Democratic candidates opposed military aid to the contras. Even a tough-talking administration has been unable to commit American troops to a shooting war for more than a few days at a time (Granada, Libya).

• Arms control is also a modal position in popular consciousness— so much so that when Reagan looked for a way to recoup his losses after a year of Iran-contra scandal, Arias-sponsored Central American talks, stalemate in Nicaragua, and Bork defeat, he resorted to an arms control deal with the evil empire. He knew that arms control would prove popular. Public sentiment in favor of arms control has been strong since the early Sixties, when it convinced John F. Kennedy to arrange detente with Khrushchev and sign the (alas, limited) test-ban treaty. When Gorbachev accepted the principle of on-site inspection, he pulled the ground out from under American objections.

4

But no sooner have these achievements been ticked off than their limits become stark:

• The underclass is in desperate straits. Housing decays; hard-core unemployment is rampant. Crime is a way of life.

• Environmental damage proceeds faster than feeble protections. Legal changes are holding actions. Environmentalist rhetoric often masks cosmetic reform.

• The arms control achieved since 1972's SALT I is far from the millennium. Reagan will leave office presiding over a larger number of nuclear weapons than he took charge of upon coming to power. Thanks to superpower laissez-faire, the nuclear contagion has reached India, Pakistan, Israel, and South Africa, with more on the way. The Star Wars fantasy remains alive, although injured.

• The localist politics and professional activism of Sixties veterans haven't built any national organization and haven't made much of a wave in national political circles. The thousands of activists who organized for civil rights and campus reform, against the war, etc. in the Sixties, and in successor movements since then (feminism, ecology, consumer rights, labor, tenants' rights, etc.) are amazingly underrepresented in the Senate, the House of Representatives, and among governors. In the professions they've established a presence—medicine, law, the academy, the media—and have an influence. In local politics, they've made possible the mayoral careers of Andrew Young, Harold Washington and Art Agnos, among others. But the typical Sixties organizer scorned electoral politics, compromising, coalitions. We preferred the wildness of the back streets to the mildness of the back rooms. So we have less power than our numbers would have suggested. And we have no institution which could multiply that power—nasty as such institutions can turn out to be in practice.

5

Gains, losses. The more you hope for, the more impressive the losses are. Is there a historical analogue which would make sense of both? A precedent which reminds us that enormous change takes its own sweet and not-so-sweet time?

The upheavals of 1789, 1848, and 1917 also culminated in retreat, reaction, recrimination, disillusion, and gloom. But one feature of these global moments, the successful and the failing and the ambiguous ones, is that when you storm heaven, the guardians at the gate storm back. You can't crash up against all the powers, accuse them of crimes against humanity, demand that they disappear, threaten to choke off their lifelines—and expect that they'll go quietly. Such innocence is fatuous. How could there be an upheaval of Sixties dimensions without a counterreaction? How could there be a Reformation without a Counter Reformation? The Reformation, remember, took decades to unfold. And the Roman Catholic Church did not go quietly. It has, in fact, survived quite handsomely. It fought back with an Inquisition—and at the same time, to a certain degree, reformed itself along lines that the Protestant reformers had agitated for. In the end, the Reformation and the Counter Reformation worked out a complicated coexistence. Fair enough. The world is too small for a titanic struggle to the death. The wonderful irony is that after all these centuries, elements of the Catholic Church emerge as forces of peace and justice.

Only supreme acumen might conceivably have carried the movements of the Sixties—in alliance with the hated liberals—to a political victory which might have dominated the decades after 1968. In the midst of furious 1968 a left-liberal coalition would have required great delicacy and diplomacy on the part of the craven Hubert Humphrey. Fat chance! That moment of possibility passed. After the Sixties' start-up Reformation, Nixon's partial Counter Reformation, and Jimmy Carter's interregnum came Ronald Reagan's counter-Sixties. Ed Meese, who catapulted to right-wing prominence when he prosecuted the Berkeley campus' Free Speech Movement in 1964, became chief law enforcer; Lowell Jensen, after prosecuting Huey Newton and the Oakland Seven, became Meese's deputy (and later a San Francisco Federal judge). Reagan, who became governor against a half-hearted liberal incumbent who couldn't manage the civil rights and student movements, became president against a half-hearted liberal incumbent who couldn't manage the Ayatollah Khomeini.

The Reagan rollback began. It has produced its own successes (not least, a military boom and, at last, a Supreme Court majority); it has also disappointed its own fanatics and bumped up against its own limits. Its high-water mark is past. With the courts as an important exception, the Reagan trance is unlikely to outlast the Reagan administration. In national politics, we find ourselves afloat in a new interregnum. The Sixties Reformation and the Counter Reformation are both alive. The values of the Sixties have another chance—embedded in women's, labor, black, Hispanic, gay, and peace movements, in which veterans of the Sixties loom large. Contrary to the "Big Chill"

legend and the promotional efforts of Jerry Rubin, the typical New Left veteran remains on the left, remains committed to the best values—if not the dotted i's and crossed t's— of the Sixties.

Success or failure, then? The disconcerting thing is that the totals can't be totted up. The legacy of our own Reformation is not a marble mausoleum. It is a commitment to move history toward life and against death, toward what is open and against what is closed: toward equality based on difference, toward the self-determination of peoples, toward the liberation of the earth from the heavy weight of the destroyers. Put this way, the legacy of the Sixties is something that remains—perpetually—to be made. In this light, the Sixties, long gone, live.

AIDS, Cultural Life, & the Arts

A Forum

CITY LIGHTS REVIEW sent to people in the arts this statement
about the impact of AIDS on cultural life:

> When government and mass media exploit the vulnerabil-
> ity of certain people with AIDS (homosexuals, Blacks, Hi-
> spanics, women in the sex industry), an oppressive
> morality is reinforced and diversity is threatened. Today, a
> community is emerging to work toward change, and artists
> and writers have been responding with their work and with
> their lives.

We asked for comment, either personal or theoretical.
What follows are some of the responses we received.

(A.S.)

DUANE MICHALS

AIDS and Imagination

First there is the World; then there is the Other World—the Other World is the place I lose myself in; in its calendar turnings: in its pre-invented existence; the barrage rush of twists and turns where sometimes I feel weary in trying to keep up with it; minute by minute adapt—the world of the stop light, the no smoking signs, the rental world, the split-rail fencing shielding hundreds of barren miles of wilderness from the human step. The place where by virtue of having been born centuries late one is denied access to earth and space; choice or movement. The bought up world; the owned world—the world of coded sounds; the world of language, the world of lies; the packaged world; the world of speed in metallic motion. The Other World where I've always felt like an alien. The Other World where one adapts and stretches its boundaries through keys of the imagination. But then the imagination is encoded with the inventions of the Other World. One stops before a light that turns from green to red and one grows centuries old in that moment. Someone once said that the Other World was run by a different species of human. It's the distance of stepping back or slowing down that reveals the Other World. It's the dislocation of response that reveals it.

This was a sensation I would experience while growing up through my teens where I could see myself from miles above the earth as if from the clouds and see this tiny human form of myself from overhead either sitting or moving through this clockwork of civilization; the huge ticking mass of it, and it all looked like something out of everyone's control; or conversely in the control of only a few; those that made up the iron cylinders of the pre-invented machine or those that threw themselves from the tops of bridges.

The Other World gets into one's bloodstream with the invisibility of a lover. It slowly takes the shape of the cells and their growth, internalized until it becomes an extension of the body. Traveling into primitive cultures allows one a sudden and clear view of the Other World; the invention of the word "Nature"—the disassociation from the ground one walks on. In growing up I was constantly aware of the sense of this in the same way one experiences a vague fear but can't distill the form of it from the table or the cup one is holding or the skies rolling between the window frames.

With the appearance of AIDS and the subsequent death of friends and neighbors I now have the recurring sensation of seeing the streets and radius of blocks before me from miles above; only now instead of focusing on the form of myself in the midst of this Other World, I see everything at once: like pressing one's eye to the earth above a small crevice from which there are streams of ants uttering from the shadows—and all of it looks amazing instead of just deathly.

At one time it was where, in the last week before I left the city to go somewhere else for a long period of time, the city suddenly changed; it was suddenly revealed to me as if I had let go of some things that were keeping it hidden; the more wonderful things tended to happen or reveal themselves in the days before departure: life or living seemed quite an amazing spectacle—there was humanity beneath every gesture moving along the sidewalks. It was a sudden vision of The World; a transient position of the body in relation to The World. So I came to understand that to give up one's environment was to also give up biography and all the encoded daily movements: the false reassurance of the railing outside the door which inadvertently locked coded information and reactions into memory. This was the beginning of a definition of The World for me. A place that might be described as interior world. The place where movement was comfortable; where boundaries were stretched or obliterated; no walls, borders, language, or fear.

With the appearance of AIDS and the sense of mortality I now find everything revealing itself to me in this way; the sense that came about in moments of departure, only now I don't even have to go anywhere—it's the possibility of departure in a final sense; a sense as in death that is now opening up the gates. Once I felt acutely alien; now it's more like immersion in a body of warm water and the water that surrounds me is air is breathing is life itself. I'm acutely aware of myself alive and witnessing; like a long-distance runner who suddenly finds himself in the solitude of distance among trees and light and the sight and sounds of friends are way back there. All behind me are the friends that died; I'm breathing this air that they can't breathe; I'm seeing this ratty monkey in a cheap Mexican circus wearing a red and blue embroidered jacket and it's collecting coins and I can reach out and touch it like they can't. And time is now compressed: I joke and say that I feel like I've taken out another six month lease on this body, on this vehicle of sound and motion, and every painting I make I make with the sense that it may be the last thing I do and so I try and pull everything in to the surface of that painting. I work quickly now and feel as if there is no time for bullshit; cut straight to the heart of the senses and map it out as clearly as tools and growth allow. And in the better moments I can see my friends; vague transparencies of their faces maybe over my shoulder or superimposed on the surface of my eyes; thus I'm more aware of myself—seeing myself see from a distance; seeing myself see others I can almost see my own breath see my internal organs functioning pump pumping—and these days I see the edge of mortality; the edge of death and dying around everything like a warm halo of light sometimes dim sometimes irradiated—I see myself seeing death; it's like a transparent celluloid image of myself is accompanying myself everywhere I go. I see my friends and I see myself and I see breath coming from my lips and chest and everything is fading; becoming a shadow that may disappear as the sun goes down.

DAVID WOJNAROWICZ

Preface: I honestly find it very difficult to assemble anything like a measured reaction because in many ways the first several years of this epidemic felt like nothing so much as having your house burn down and the neighbors turn out to hose gasoline on it. The situation in New York has been especially depressing because the epidemic has generated no unanimous sense of civic catastrophe; when certain people lament that the bulk of cases are now among IV drug users, poor Blacks, and Hispanics, I sometimes sense that they're secretly relieved, imagining the problem will become a problem of "the Other" for them as it has been for "the general population." At the same time, groups like ACT UP and organizations like GMHC have given many people in all "risk groups" an authentic and powerful conviction of solidarity, and my hope is that this will outlive the epidemic and incite demands for social equity, including a national health system that doesn't require a choice between your money and your life. But this is only a hope. Not a single presidential candidate has prioritized AIDS as a primary concern in the course of his campaign.

I don't think the epidemic and the people it's taken away have been out of my mind for more than a few minutes for at least four years now. There was a period when almost every week, and then almost every day, someone I knew was reported sick or dead. Lately it's been less frequent. I honestly can't picture the effect of acquired immune deficiency on the culture. Culture arises from what people are. Many noble things may come from individuals; from the industrial zone that gives us our magazines and television shows we can't expect anything but reductive exploitation and an occasional burst of crocodile tears over the "most innocent victims," i.e., babies and transfusion cases. The sad thing about mass culture is its relentless degradation of life into cheap entertainment. If the mass media had dealt with AIDS as a medical emergency and not chased after every "moral" phobia attached to a spokesperson, thousands of instances of persecution might not have occurred. (One of the most pathetic spectacles I've ever seen was a fag-baiting picket line outside the St. Mark's Baths composed of working-class Black men and Orthodox Jews: all these people who, if they ever open the camps, will find themselves right in there with the rest of us.)

For people fortunate enough to survive this period, it's going to be important to remember exactly what happened. This is not like the polio epidemic, not like TB and all the other things it's been compared to. It's an epidemic whose afflicted people have been hatefully persecuted and blamed for their own sufferings, a litmus test of people's humanity.

GARY INDIANA

My gay friends in the arts do not talk to me at length about their friends, dying or dead from AIDS. But a friend will say on the phone, "I must go now. I have to call _____ at the hospital who is dying of AIDS." The casualness of the statement sends chills down my spine. Of course this casualness masks the grief, the pain, the horror, the fear. Once in a while I ask about _____, a playwright, or _____, a poet, only to learn that he is dead from AIDS. I feel as though an off-stage war is taking place: victims fall behind the curtain while those on stage read their lines, the same lines over and over: "I must go now . . . "

ROBERTA ALLEN

SUE COE

AIDS and Responsible Drug Education

On January 29th, I publicly defied New York State law by distributing sixteen disposable syringes and needles on the Lower East Side. Police, who had been notified, were present, but did not arrest me. This act of defiance was reported in only one paper, *Newsday*, two days later. Ironically, it was the same day the governor's office reversed its position and said it would permit public and private agencies in New York City to go forward with a plan to distribute sterilized syringes and needles to addicts. Dr. Stephen Joseph, the city's health commissioner, state health officials, and the private group ADAPT should be commended for their courage in pushing such a program forward. These efforts give a measure of official sanction and a mile of public awareness to two well-established medical facts: 1. Heroin addiction is an illness extremely difficult to "cure." 2. Most heroin deaths are not due to so-called "overdoses" but to diseases transmitted by shared or repeatedly used needles. The first fact makes the "Just Say NO" campaign about as simplistic as a "Just Cheer UP" campaign for chronic depression. The second fact was well documented over sixteen years ago by the Consumer Union Report on Licit and Illicit Drugs. Even common sense tells us that people can "overdose" on virtually any substance, e.g., water (drowning), food (bulimia), or even air (air-swallowers gulping air into their stomachs). Of course, the British National Health Services established and accepted these facts 55 years ago. AIDS and AIDS research is simply allowing information well chronicled in science a chance to reach a public badly misinformed about addiction.

Unfortunately, this program of exchanging dirty needles for sterilized ones does not go far enough. Two hundred addicts will be allowed to enter the program, out of a population of 200,000 with 40–50% infected. Neither do the Europeans who have legalized the sale of disposable syringes and needles. In the life of today's typical heroin addict the idea of exchangeable or disposable needles seems to vanish at the moment of injection. Besides, complicated restrictions involving strict identification, including fingerprinting, will severely limit the number of addicts who will actually participate. There exists a simple easy-to-do health prevention technique with better chance of success. Addicts can do a pretty good job of sterilizing their "works" by flushing the syringe twice with common household liquid bleach, then rinsing twice in the same manner with fresh water. The glass of bleach and the glass of water should then be thrown away after each usage.

The only city in America that is effectively distributing such information is San Francisco, although Seattle and Washington, D.C. are now following with similar programs. Instigated by the Haight-Ashbury Free Medical Clinic and expanded by the Mid-City Consortium to combat AIDS, this campaign has been remarkably successful in a very short time.

In a paper presented last June at the Third International Conference on AIDS, John K. Watters, director of San Francisco's Urban Health Study, reported on a one-year evaluation of the impact made by street-based distribution of this information. In 1986 (before the program), only 3% of Intravenous Drug Users (IVDUs) surveyed mentioned bleach in connection with needle cleaning. By contrast, after one year of the program, 68% of the IVDUs reported using bleach to decontaminate needles and syringes. Also, instead of only 3% knowing such a simple easy technique was possible, 91% of the IVDUs stated that they now knew bleach could be helpful in killing AIDS virus being spread by dirty needles. There are many aspects of the study important to discuss, but space permits mention of only a few. Obviously, major advantages of this experimental program were anonymity, a high impact by a small cadre of health workers taking it to the streets, and the role word-of-mouth information played. Less effective was the dissemination of information via the mass media (i.e., articles such as this).

Also important was the fact that the entire Mid-City program cost only $270,000 for its first year of operation. There is some hint that this program is having an effect on curbing the spread of AIDS, but it's much too early to make the connection scientifically. Common sense, however, says the effort is worth a serious try. The spread of AIDS via needles by IVDUs in New York City is well recognized as much higher than San Francisco. The quicker we start to recognize that we are dealing with a serious health problem and not a moral issue, the quicker we can begin implementing solutions that will work. In the Middle Ages over a period of 200 years, one-third of the known world population was wiped out by the plague three times. Throughout most of this period many doctors (and even some common folk songs) mentioned that rats and lice were chiefly responsible for the spread of the disease. Why it took 200 years for the powers that be to accept this fact and institute corrective measures is now quite obvious. All sorts of superstitions instigated by public moralists got in the way. Witches, Jews, the devil, even listening to evil music, were at one time or another blamed.

In six centuries, it's astonishing that we haven't learned all that much. AIDS is just starting to allow us to consider responsible sex education; at some point we must also consider responsible drug education. If we want to save lives first and worry about souls second, medical science and common sense must come to the front while preachers and politicians step to the rear.

ABBIE HOFFMAN

"Hi. How're doing?
Why don't you tell me what you look like!"
"Oh, I'm about 170 pounds . . . . . . "

These men are enjoying the Party Line, the only conference line in
New York for men only.   Just dial 100-411-700-777-7070, and
you'll be connected. An ongoing encounter with men of all different
interests: young or old, top or bottom . . . they're all here. It's erotic, safe, and billed discreetly on your telephone bill. Only 89 cents
per minute.

Los Angeles, Chicago, Miami, and now the hottest 24 hour Party
Line comes to New York. The party never stops, it just gets better
and better. Only 95 cents for the first minute, and 45 cents for each
additional minutes. Live action . . . Action as lively or as heavy as
you want to make it. Call 1-900-999-1114. Or try our free line first
. . . 643-1200 or 643-1201.

At Man Talk, we talk tough and listen hard.   1-900-999-4600.
95 cents for the first minute and 45 cents for each additional minutes. Available in area codes 212, 516, 718, 914 and in New Jersey
201. Man Talk.

A survey of 129 television shows (232 half-hour segments) broadcast over the three major networks during the opening week of the 1987-1988 season reported 65,000 sexual references appearing during the prime afternoon and evening hours. In a *New York Times* report of the survey ("Study Finds Barrage of Sex on TV," 27 January 1988) it is indicated that's an average of 27 references an hour, including 9 kisses, 5 hugs, 10 sexual innuendos, and between 1 and 2 references each to sexual intercourse and to "deviant or discouraged sexual practices." According to the *New York Times* writer, the researchers had to resort to fractions when counting reference to birth control, sexually transmitted diseases and sex education. The study found no advertisement for contraceptive products or services, nor a need to balance the prime-time references with messages about the consequences of sexual behavior. Neglected in the study was any discussion of the role of the Catholic Church and other fundamentalist denominations as the prime pressure groups in keeping condom ads off network television.

(Study conducted by Lou Harris & Associates for the Planned Parenthood Federation of America. Released January 26, 1988.)

© 1988 - DARA BIRNBAUM

All television material presented was recorded from Manhattan Cable TV Channel J, New York City after midnight on the dates of March 27, March 28 and April 10, 1988.

"Amber Lynn, I call your line everyday,
you're incredible. . .
Are you going to suck my cock?"

"Is that what you want?
Do you want Amber Lynn to suck your cock?
I will fulfill all your dreams. . .
With my mouth."

Geisha To Go has more young, beautiful, and exotic girls. Every month from all parts of the Orient they come here to delight as only our geishas can. 24 hours a day we can come to you within a few minutes . . . Phone us now 496-8186 . . . 496-8186 . . . New geishas want to meet you.

Whether you're at work or at play . . . Whether you stay in or go out . . . Attache Escorts is your model company . . . Our models are the perfect picture to fulfill your every need and fantasy . . . And when your need arises, we'll arise to every occasion . . . . Attache ladies will come wherever you are . . . We're only a phone call away. Just call "HEY"-6400, dial H-E-Y-6-4-0-0 for Attache.

"So beautiful . . . so aromatic . . .
I'm going to rip your fucking head off . . .
This is what you really want . . ."
(whipping air)

I'd die before I'd hurt you . . .
So die sucker . . .

Fuck that shit!
Just call me."

Oriental Outcall. In the mysterious East from monarchies where men are king . . . obedient girls trained in pleasure are available day and night. Phone 744-6207 . . . 744-6207 . . . Phone Emperor's Oriental Outcall and reign over the beauties of the East.

"I'm so lonely.
O-o-o-o . . .
That's it . . . That's it . . .
You can pick me up anytime. . ."

DARA BIRNBAUM

A Speech Presented to the Senate Judiciary Committee:

Voting on legislation requiring mandatory HIV antibody tests for anyone convicted of prostitution; and other legislation making it a felony for prostitutes knowing they are HIV antibody positive to provide sexual services.

Gentlemen, There must be, I hope, one or two of you who is still sitting on the fence about the mandatory HIV testing of prostitutes. It's rare that prostitutes can speak for themselves on these matters. As a result, you couldn't exactly say we have much representation. I am a prostitute. I provide safe sexual services to men exactly like yourselves. I know that most of you have brothers, cousins, and golf partners who have partaken of the services of prostitutes. I know there are others of you who have used our services. It's common practice to use us and discard us and our rights afterwards—men have the power in this world—so I can only appeal to your sense of justice and chivalry in hopes that you still have some conscience left after devoting your lives to a career that is certainly more hypocritical and corrupt than my career.

As a working prostitute of ten years, having known hundreds of prostitutes, even before the crisis, I know that prostitutes in massage parlors and on the streets use condoms. There was always and is now extreme peer pressure to use condoms. Prostitutes want to use them. Without them, it's incredibly messy and unhealthy, and was so even before AIDS. In addition, most prostitutes I know have gotten tested; counseling and anonymous testing can be a great service to our community. As you know, prostitute activists are eager to protect our health and the health of our clients.

I have encountered disgusting clients who try to bully and insult me into having sex without a condom. These men are surely committing crimes against their wives. Now I hear that you want to punish us for spreading disease. Coercing or bribing a person into not using a condom should be a crime.

Last year Senator Roberti sponsored a bill that makes agreeing to commit prostitution a crime. Obviously this law legalizes entrapment, a shocking violation of our rights. And now we have these bills for mandatory HIV testing, and for making it a felony for HIV antibody positive prostitutes to provide sexual services, even if these practices are completely safe (i.e. manual stimulation). Many of you understand these hypocrisies, yet believe that the punishment of prostitutes in an appropriate symbol and tactic. It certainly is traditional. Some of you have confided to me that it's very important to ensure a clean group of prostitutes because after all, boys will be boys. The legislative tactics of AB2319 seem designed to ensure that there are clean women to use, at the expense of those who will be quarantined. Naturally, this method of curtailing the spread of AIDS is ineffective. There is not enough money to fund the vice squad to entrap the HIV-positive prostitutes. A COYOTE study indicates that vice cops often have sex with prostitutes in exchange for protection, before and after arrests. This legislation results in greater funding for vice cops, a group of men who express themselves (i.e., power) sexually, by means of relations with prostitutes. Your legislative aides with whom I've discussed these details agree that this is an institutionalized form of rape.

Cheaper than arrests, cheaper than salaries for the rapists with badges, would be education, job training, disability payments, IV drug recovery programs, and a needle exchange program as New York has. I am deeply concerned with the fate of people of color—globally and nationally—who will bear the brunt of this crisis with the gay community. Do you realize that black women, who represent a minority of prostitutes, are the ones who will be affected by this legislation? Already a large majority of the women prison population is black. Poverty and IV drug addiction force poor women into prostitution. And I want to express my alarm at the effects of this legislation on women who have been raped as children, who really have little choice but prostitution, women who are victims of men who prey on their victimization.

Finally, regarding the under-the-table parlaying that resulted in this bill, this crime against women, a bill that is an absurd and inexcusable sellout by Assemblyman Bronzan, who has privately confessed that he does not like this legislation, but was coerced into constructing it to protect the power of Willie Brown and his particular brand of liberalism which, as we see from his strategies regarding abortion and reproductive rights, places women's issues at a low priority.

Your vote today will influence the tide of the nation about the registry and quarantine of victims of the AIDS crisis. I must implore you on this committee to hesitate before allowing such legislation to sweep the country. I implore you to do what you can to stop a dangerous situation and to act courageously. I hope some of you can understand that the special circumstances of this epidemic—including our knowledge of prevention and the familiarity we should have with the history of genocide—must prevent your passing this bill, which in my book would be a far greater crime than any blow job I've ever given.

CAROL LEIGH aka SCARLOT HARLOT

Arthur Rimbaud was Homosexual

The national flag suits a diseased landscape.
Our scatology'll drown their militaristic tongues;
In our urban decay we'll sustain the most emotionless
     prostitution; we'll murder all liberal revolt.
On to the filthiest sexual lands!—in the service of a really
     monstrous industrial and militaristic exploitation.
Until you and I meet again—it doesn't matter where. *Conscripts*
     of our own will. We have a ferocious philosophy.
We ignorant of logic facts pigs for pleasure—death to the society that is!
This is real progress! Forward, march.

                                           —*after Rimbaud*

Why do people hate homosexuals? Who are the people who hate homosexuals? What are the relations between sexuality and politics?

    The poet, elsewhere, not in our Western society today, was the speaker and guide of his or her community. Partly because of his homosexuality Rimbaud was one of the first poets in this Western society who fully understood that he was alienated from his society.

    Above all Arthur Rimbaud hated hypocrisy, the deadness of the provincial bourgeois society into which he had been born. He wanted to go to a world that was pagan, a world in which politics sexuality language sensation and identity are interconnected.

    Rimbaud saw that this society separates. It separates politics and power from sexuality, politics from poetry and vision. It separates people from each other according to their sexual characters, colors, and classes. This society, which controls by separation, is a society of death.

THE PEOPLE WHO HATE HOMOSEXUALS ARE PARTLY CORRECT: SEXUALITY DOES NOT OCCUR ONLY IN THE BED.
SEXUALITY AND LIFE AND DEATH ARE INTERCONNECTED. IT IS ONLY A SOCIETY OF DEATH WHICH SEPARATES DEATH FROM LIFE AND FETISHIZES DEATH.
THIS GOVERNMENT IS TRYING TO FETISHIZE AIDS, NOT DEAL WITH IT.

KATHY ACKER

Exploitation of the vulnerable by political institutions and "information" media in our culture is nothing new. But the tactics employed by such forces in the face of the burgeoning AIDS epidemic border on genocide, if they are not, in fact, evidence of deliberate extermination of members of "undesirable" minority groups outside the so-called "mainstream" or "general" population.

With respect to the gay/homosexual/bisexual male population (and I suppose I refer here primarily to white males, given the reluctance of many men in ethnic minority communities who engage in sex with other men to identify themselves as gay or even homosexual), there has been unleashed since the early 1980s a sexual repression right out of Orwell's *1984* and Oceania's Anti Sex League. After more than a decade of heartening progress, the gay movement has encountered the same old oppression in the new, more powerful (and frightening) guise of protecting the physical as well as the moral and spiritual health of the nation. This oppression has rivalled not only McCarthyism but even Nazism, as the specter of mass quarantining of homosexuals, for their own benefit much less than that of the "healthy mainstream," has been repeatedly raised. A "public health" measure that mandates reportability of HIV infection and permits quarantining has even been placed on the ballot in California. Twice, now.

The freedom of literary expression in and of matters pertaining to sex has been severely compromised in recent years. One gay writer has felt the need to announce (on the verso of its title page) that his novel is set before the onset of the epidemic and that he no longer liberally exchanges bodily fluids. Gay Men's Press in London, itself the victim of harassment and intimidation on the part of conservative religious and political forces, remarked in a letter to me that GMP was turning down my novella *Nighttime* partly "because it's a bit difficult to find a home *for such work* [emphasis mine] these days, post-AIDS." (Though deliberately erotic, *Nighttime* contains one, briefly described sex scene, in which the infamous bodily fluids are not mentioned, not that I need to defend my fiction against any censor.)

Any attack on desire, let alone on the description of sex, is an invasion of the mind of the individual and of its sacred privacy. Erotic and sexual imaginings and thoughts are the very basis not only of human art but of humanity itself. Attempts to repress eroticism in Western civilization, for example, when the Church shut down the Renaissance with the edicts that created the Counter-Reformation and enforced thought control with the Office of the Holy Inquisition, have created centuries of human suffering and cruelty, twisting desire that affirms life into desire that destroys it. Physical torture, maiming, and extermination of countless individuals have always accompanied the efforts of the thought police, whatever their religious and/or political ideology.

Paradoxically, gay artists and writers are flourishing bravely during the current repression as never before in this country. The NAMES Project Quilt is but the most powerful and visible expression of love and desire in the face of bigotry and death. The plays and other performed writing that the FCC is trying to keep off the air, the poetry, fiction, essays, and autobiographies that gay writers continue to craft during our Holocaust: all represent artifacts that help us think and feel our various ways through this dangerous period in all of our lives, while also recording our ordeal for those who will follow us.

But none of these creations will have very long lives if Orwellian attacks on homosexual desire and sexual expression succeed in igniting the rage and panic of the "general population" the government and media purport to speak for.

Desire cannot be annihilated, but expression can be thwarted and silenced. Puritans have burned libraries, destroyed printing presses, closed theaters, and obliterated images throughout Western history. Artists and writers, whose special role has always been to create beauty while exploring meaning, ignore puritans and censors not only at their own peril but at that of all their fellow humans as well.

And these days, in the face of the AIDS epidemic, the peril is mortal in virtually every way.

JACK COLLINS

from

The Return of Unnatural Acts:
Notes for a Genealogy of Safe Sex

AIDS words—the linguistic constructs used to talk about AIDS—are never "factual" or "truths," but take on particular meanings at particular times, and are understood differently by different people. The challenge to AIDS organizers is to understand how much information and how much disinformation is conveyed by each term at any given point. For example, "body fluids" is a useful term—it highlights the importance of biological transportation, the active movement of infected fluid from one body to another. While it is less specific than saying "semen and blood," it also escapes the ways in which both semen and blood in this culture have heavy moral baggage—both are already constructed as venal, fatal fluids. An attempt to reconstruct the meanings that were given to safe sex in different phases of the AIDS crisis gives us some guidelines for resisting sex phobia and homophobia as we devise a "medically safe" sex and politically powerful sexual liberation.

In a highly articulated urban gay male culture, there were intersecting discourses about sex. There was sexual identity (leather man to disco queen), which implied a rich terrain of sexual possibilities within the category "gay;" there was sexual practice (what acts men engaged in); and sexual location. This was the fantastic world of possibilities for those gay men; this was the economy of pleasures and representations in which their sex was negotiated.

One of the most interesting artifacts developed in this culture was the hanky code, an expanding semiotic using bandanas of different colors to indicate the specific preferences of individual men. While this has been viewed as a commodification of sex, it was also the embodiment of a sexual ethic. On a practical level, use of the code avoided the problem of getting home with a person of noncompatible practices. But even more, the hanky code rested on the assumption that sex was to be negotiated between rough equals. Choosing a hanky or hankies drew identity and practice together in an articulation of who one was sexually and how one expected to enact sex. In Foucaultian terms, the hanky code was a discourse about the care of the self. (In contrast, heterosexuals had little strong sense of self as "heterosexual," and functioned under an implied code in which vaginal intercourse was the paradigmatic practice, and in which women negotiated as inferiors.)

This is the sexual semiology into which the first information about safe sex arrived. In the days before "The Test," the urban gay male sexual ethic rested on a presumption of infection, requiring everyone to protect others and oneself from further infection, or infection with possible co-factors. The first pamphlets—like *How to Have Sex in an Epidemic*—tried to reinforce the broad range of practices engaged in by gay men, but at the same time to get men to think about making specific, transmission inter-rupting modifications in those practices.

Some time in 1984, the safe sex hanky code was invented by AIDS groups in Texas. This reversed the previous understanding of the relation-ship between safety and the multiplicity of practices. The idea of this hanky code made safe sex a positive choice rather than a limitation, and laid the groundwork for constructing a notion of self—and identity—around safe sex: "I demand (am) safe sex."

Then came Heterosexual AIDS Panic, Phase One, in late 1984, which recast the notion of safe sex in two ways: it strongly promoted the idea that there are safe people (true heterosexuals) and dangerous people (closeted gay men, bisexuals, IV drug users, prostitutes); and since, among hetero-sexuals, intercourse is hegemonic, safe sex was made to mean abstinence, monogamy or condoms. On the rare occasions when nonpenetrative means to heterosexual orgasm were discussed, they were posed as "alterna-tives" to the "real thing." This insistence that intercourse is the real sex soon spilled over into gay safe sex literature as well, as the condom became the big controversy in 1986/87. Safe sex discussions now began with a dis-cussion of the importance of condoms, and then discussed the range of "other possibilities" for a fulfilling sex life.

Then arrived the so-called AIDS test, which is more properly called the HIV antibody test, because it does not test for the virus believed to cause AIDS and is not diagnostic for AIDS. In fact, it doesn't actually look for the "antibody" to HIV but detects certain proteins which, in North Americans, appear in the bodies of people who have mounted a response to HIV. The two procedures which give a negative or positive reading are called ELISA or Western Blot, with ELISA being more commonly used in the vast and proliferating testing industry.

This understanding of the biological ecology of health is totally ab-sent in the massive implementation of ELISA in the so-called Alternative Testing Sites (federally and state funded). The ATS created a new under-standing of safe sex—one which identified as safe any act between people who "are" negative, and as unsafe, sexual contact with people who "are" positive, according to the "test." Now people, rather than acts, define what is safe sex. The discourse of safe sex thus becomes involved in con-structing identities around infection or presumption of infection, instead of focusing—as in the early years—on the biology of transmission, on the technology of safe sex, and on the practice of safe sex. Safe sex becomes a symbol of danger and safety, with ELISA as an indicator of safe versus dan-gerous persons. Safe sex ceases to be a practice of sexual pleasure, and be-comes an avoidance of sexual danger.

Masters and Johnson in *Crisis: Heterosexual Behavior in the Age of*

AIDS (1988), articulate the most bizarre idea of safe sex versus natural sex. Their attitude projects a deep-seated fear about the cultural danger of safe sex:

> Sex partners of uncertain (HIV anti-body) testing status (could) . . . wear disposable plastic gloves during all intimate moments. These gloves, after all, aren't too different from condoms. Yet we are unwilling to seriously entertain such an outlandish notion—right now, it seems so unnatural and artificial as to violate the essential dignity of humanity.

They willingly ignore the difference between creating "intimate moments" and the practical realities of transmission: the point is not to wrap oneself in a latex barrier at the moment of sexual transcendence, but to don appropriate accoutrements before sticking a finger with cuts or sores into an asshole or vagina.

The old hanky code, and the wide range of identities, sites, and practices of sex it implied, viewed sex as perverse, fragmented, a montage of inchoate desires, objects charged with symbolism, and unexpected orderings of the sexual drama. Masters and Johnson imply that safe sex is unnatural, and that "natural sex," in their view—intercourse between ELISA negatives—is safe. Lost is any notion that acts, not people or transcendence, create the condition that allows HIV to move from point A to point B.

It is the current construction of natural sex that is the site of our resistance today: in a safe sex discourse that states that "safe people" (as determined by ELISA) can have sex naturally, the rest of us—those of us who "fail" or simply refuse to "take the test"—are doomed to a purgatory where our sexuality—and ourselves—are represented as dehumanized and expendable.

CINDY PATTON

Nationally-known illustrator Lynda Barry prepared these illustrations for the Northwest AIDS Foundation's BE WELL EQUIPPED safer-sex education campaign.

BE WELL EQUIPPED.
The Northwest AIDS Foundation

LYNDA BARRY

Literature in the Age of AIDS

When I sat down to work on a new novel I realized that it would be absolutely impossible to write about anything but the AIDS crisis. It is so totally present. As a person living in America I am inundated with the dominant culture's hysterical distortions about AIDS every single day. Yet, as a lesbian living in New York's Lower East Side, the real story unfolds in front of me. Television, as always, is primarily concerned with the protection of heterosexual white men, those least at risk. The evening news reports congressmen dying of "blood transfusions." One of the greatest living forces behind the hatred and isolation of homosexuals, Cardinal O'Conner, is appointed to President Reagan's AIDS commission. We live in the United States of Denial. At the same time I watch the truth on display in my own backyard. Gay men get sick and die and no one cares. Their lovers are evicted from their apartments. *The New York Times* reports they are survived by their parents. Black and Latin drug users and their lovers die and no one notices at all. Some lives are more important than others. Some deaths are shocking. Some invisible.

When I started writing *People in Trouble*, I resolutely refused to produce a book principally concerned with watching one or more characters slowly deteriorate and die over the course of three hundred pages. Instead I have decided to focus on AIDS activism: the decision by those at risk to unite in anger and dedicate themselves to direct action to stop the AIDS crisis. For AIDS is the disaster of my generation. It is our holocaust, our civil war, our blacklist, our Vietnam. We will be spending the rest of lives trying to understand what happened, trying to recover, trying to avenge the unnecessary suffering caused by the neglect and contempt of our neighbors, families, and government.

There will be a time, though, when revisionism and sentimentality will drive some to ask "Where were you during the AIDS crisis?" "What did you do?" For those of us who expect to live to that day, the purposefulness and dignity of our individual lives will be determined then by how we behave now. Activist organizations like New York City's ACT UP (AIDS Coalition to Unleash Power) are doing what gay people have always done in this world—defiantly, proudly, in community, take care of the situation ourselves, in the face of contempt and great pain. These are the places where people must make their stand. These are the acts of great courage that I hope will appear in the literature of AIDS, which can be a literature of empowerment and strength.

SARAH SCHULMAN

The Rape of AIDS:
Some Questions

How will this penetrating plague
deflower our erotic life?

No more rakes, libertines or swingers?
  Only candidates for the seminary?
No more abusing of alien substances?
  Only self-abuse?
No more gay dogs, gay deceivers or dirty old men?
  Only pussycats, flagellants and old maids?
No more exchanging of vital fluids?
  Only soft drinks and tea for two?
No more pickups, procurers or gigolos?
  Only hermits and couch potatoes?
No more intimate contact with the real thing?
  Only scrabble, frisbee and high mindedness?
No more dirty novels or filthy pictures?
  Only abstract art and cookbooks?

Is it back to the closet? Back to the cave?
Back into the dark untouchable future
accompanied by cries of woe
and laments for the dead?

JAMES BROUGHTON

from

After the Howl

III

Robert Douglas! you cannot die now!
  you are more magnetic more blunt more vibrant than I am
I will not let you die Allen Meyer
  born 1949 died March 1986
  illustrating maps to a painter's eerie dimension
I will not let you die Chuck Solomon
  born 1946 died December 1986
  deflating crimes against nature with a hoary fairy monologue
I will not let you die Esther John Sturgeon
  born 1948 died October 1983
  greeting autumn dancing on the belly of the equinox
I will not let you die Drew Lubarsky
  born 1950 died November 1984
  leading a chorus of simple WASP madmen to Oedipal glory
I will not let you die Ken Horne
  born 1943 died November 1981
  gaining recognition as San Francisco's first man diagnosed with KS,
    the innocent tragic beginning
I will not let you die Alfred Gonzales
  born 1954 died November 1986
  cross-hatching Angels over the Alamo
I will not let you die Paula McDonald
  born 1962 died June 1987
  sleeping with a bivalve man who kissed and said goodbye
I will not let you die Michael Calvert
  born 1958 died January 1987
  crafting floral epithets into bouquets of people poems for AIDS
    commiseration
I will not let you die Leonard Matlovitch
  born 1944 died June 1988
  storming the ramparts of the armed forces' double standard winning
    reinstatement and national notoriety. On your tombstone your
    chosen words are engraved: They gave him a medal for killing two
    men and a discharge for loving one.
I will not let you die Philip-Dimitri Galas
  born 1949 died August 1986
  scripting Mona Rogers' punk belligerence in your sister's chic
    pettycoats, dressing the stage with Performance Hell
I will not let you die Jon Sims
  born 1948 died July 1984

perfecting hundreds of parades twirling baton boys out of tubas and
   goose-stepping sequined underwear flags onto the seats of your
   marching trombone band
I will not let you die Michael Bennett
   born 1943 died July 1987
   finding refining polishing the stories of our lives on the Great White
   Way
I will not let you die Bob Monhaupt
   born 1949 died May 1988
   floating buck naked in an azure summer pool wrapping your winter
   woes in a hot Ruben sandwich not really flagging as your body
   failed but refusing to tell us what we already knew
I will not let you die Matsuko Iyedo
   born 1963 died September 1985
   emptying the human wastebasket engendered by shared IV needle
   cosmic drug dreams
I will not let you die Patrick Cowley
   born 1950 died November 1982
   mastering Sylvester's upper limbo Queen Anne vocals with
   synthesized disco heat synapses
I will not let you die Charles Ludlum
   born 1943 died May 1987
   creating quick-change thunder phantoms nestled in Sheridan Square
   collecting Obies for ridiculous obsessions
I will not let you die Ed Mock
   born 1938 died April 1986
   displaying black and white passion in reconverted warehouses,
   choreographic mirrors installed to induce magic motion missives
   of mime myth and celebration
I will not let you die Layton Mullins
   born 1981 died May 1987
   smiling laughing crying such sweet smiling you won't ever
   understand your own hemophiliac suffering only caring to please
   with your final forty pound smile
I will not let you die Joah Lowe
   born 1953 died January 1988
   introducing the charmed Kabuki omnigata to the savage gestures of
   modern dance hunting the wildest beauty in the world
I will not let you die Rob Gerstein
   born 1946 died April 1987
   building and fingering Baird's puppets imbuing them with flames of
   your own flaring hair, resting now waiting in memories' depths of
   Kolbein's fjords
I will not let you die James Roy Howell
   born 1936 died October 1982
   musing on Juilliard's ivory impetus unraveling woolen warmups in
   Joffrey's studio inspiring Arpino's vaulted Round of Angels

I will not let you die Michael Frigo
> born 1955 died February 1985
> compiling safe sex data from deathly aware probings recording
>> about-turn changes in our post-AIDS lifestyles

I will not let you die Edwin "Ted" Flath
> born 1930 died September 1987
> conducting Bach's assimilation into California society

I will not let you die Jerry Smith
> born 1943 died October 1986
> pounding pitons of public honesty into homophobic football faces
>> climbing brutal guide ropes planting your gay Redskins pennant at
>> the peak

I will not let you die Allan Estes
> born 1955 died May 1984
> professing theatre as Rhinoceros and grappling with that one thick
>> horn 'til it gored out the truth

I will not let you die Gerald Pearson
> born 1942 died July 1987
> pinning back the wings of the tabernacle soaring over Brigham
>> Young's head to Tivoli

I will not let you die Sam D'Allesandro
> born 1956 died February 1988
> slipping a mirage of sins past yellow silk uncertainty not waiting for
>> death's definition just stopping mid-reel

I will not let you die Bill Kraus
> born 1948 died January 1986
> championing our right to life not a sexual fascist as some vindictive
>> souls called you, but able to squeeze blood money out of Reagan's
>> indifferent turnip budget cutters

I will not let you die Dr. Tom Waddell
> born 1936 died July 1987
> bearing the Gay Games torch under hypocritic USOC single file
>> gunfire exulting Olympic! unofficial! Olympic! spiritual! Olympic!

I will not let you die Bill Kendall
> born 1949 died May 1984
> silver-plating sand dunes for Beach Blanket Babylon Goes to Heaven
>> wisking Mr. Peanut off the factory tower and etching his odd
>> elegant earthy grin, monocle and top hat ever leading you to
>> jaunty tap step floors

I will not let you die Sutter Marin
> born 1926 died June 1985
> terrorizing the denizens of south of Market rest stops waiting in
>> demon-poet ambush and yanking open the door inviting Out to
>> come in

Berkeley 1987/88   **SAM AMBLER**

Diagnosis

CHARLES SEXTON

A young man and woman, both in their twenties, invited me out to lunch when I was in San Francisco last spring. Both had AIDS and both looked wonderful, although the young man thought he must be near the end. He'd had the pneumonia twice and had been so profoundly enmeshed in the dementia a year back that he hadn't been able to recall what you needed to speak to other human beings—words or numbers?

AZT had brought him out of that, but he didn't think he could continue taking it for more than an additional three months. The young woman wore a big button saying, "PWA— Handle with Care." The waitress didn't bat an eyelash; perhaps she thought it meant my friend was a prisoner of the war in Algeria.

"No, no," my friend said. "People here are very savvy. San Francisco's the only city in the world where you can eat your supper in peace with lesions on your face."

The warmth of the day was an earnest of the summer to come. The young man drove us to Golden Gate Park in his ancient Austin-Martin. It was all that he still owned and he was very proud of it. When I told him I was positive he said, "Your time will come very soon. You must make your plans now. And don't let your plans depend on anyone else. My lover of six years dumped me a month after my diagnosis—very painful for him, no doubt, the poor dear. I was the best hairburner in town but they let me go—when I missed a few days the clients started to worry. Now I live here in San Francisco in a hospice. The other guys are a little jealous of me because I'm the only presentable one."

It was true he was beautiful, smiling, inquisitive, with the sort of shining brown hair that feels and falls like the silk fringe on the end of an opera scarf. All three of us kept bumping into one another and smiling with some pleasure, as though our dormant energies were being refired by the solar energy pulsing through us.

We walked along the crowded paths of the Japanese tea garden and in a blurred way looked at the stunted trees cantilevered out over the still pond or the visitors sardined inside the tea pavilion. Japanese tourists were taking photos of each other in the showers of cherry blossoms falling all around them. I felt a bit as though I were on coasters, seeing everything but protected by a lens. Maybe we felt the way ghosts feel when they revisit the earth: colors aren't quite true and the surrounding happiness looks somewhat staged.

Outside the garden we found a clearing in the sunny woods where we could sit. We worried a second about sitting on the possibly cold or damp ground but we bit back little smiles of medical embarrassment and gave into the pleasure of breathing the smells of the reawakening world.

My two companions expressed a joy as bitter and effervescent as tonic water, as though they were drinking in this last, this very last day. They complained about the AZT alarms going off all night at the hospice, beeping and keeping them awake. The young woman complained of government restrictions and talked pharmacology until she caught my eye and said, "It's all alphabet soup to you, isn't it?"

"Sort of."

"Right." An inhaled down beat. "Next subject."

Our excited silence became the subject, one that bordered on hysteria and reminded me of those neuron-crackling silences of my adolescence, except that back then I'd stayed silent near my lovers out of an excess of longing and a fear of offending, whereas now we had no future to worry about, just the plenitude of the moment.

The young man told me he was packing up his Austin-Martin and moving home to the lakeside village where he'd been a child. "That's what I want to see when I croak—the lake. You have to choose what your last moment will be. Start planning now. I'm serious, Ed."

Extraordinarily there was no anguish or resentment in what he was saying. Not even his realism could be called grim. When he said goodbye, as I hopped out of the car and went into City Lights to do a book signing, he said, "So long for this life." He was the second person who'd said something along those lines in a week.

EDMUND WHITE

There are simply fewer artists. Already that's a fact. The gossip strikes and suddenly we all know that so and so has it, he's spotted a few times out in public and next thing you know it's time for the memorial service. Everyone shows up and it's amazing to discover how far-reaching this person's connections and influences were and then we all go home a little poorer. I remember reading in relation to the mosaics that so predominate the visuals in Venice that the reason that art declined was that whole schools of artisans were wiped out by a plague.

This year, and by year I'm thinking since fall of '87, there seems to have been fewer deaths, and more hope—if not for a cure then for more preventative or stabilizing approaches. Also there's been more conscious inclusion of AIDS-related materials in new art. Too hard to ignore, AIDS awareness is beginning to be the most concrete definition of what's political in art.

One of the last big art auctions in New York was a benefit for GMHC. AIDS is the only issue that most artists great and small can agree is significant. It's about the human loss that artists as a group are experiencing. I can't help feeling that a sense of community is developing among artists. I attended a memorial service last summer that was not AIDS-related and the rabbi explained our collective presence there as what we know how to do. We were sad, and what human beings know how to do is come together. As the century ends and this devastating disease randomly takes among its victims people we know and love a new sense of the fragility and tenderness of life is unavoidable and growing and could be the mainstay of a more compassionate art in the next century.

EILEEN MYLES

HIV 1986–88

A small ache harasses my chest—I've wondered for months if it's muscle tension or a virus. It is my chest or this office that houses so much trouble? I sit on a card chair, cross my legs, and glance at the other men, studiously incurious; I inhale wicked institutional cheer and exhale collective anxiety. I'm taking the HIV test because my desire to know if I've contracted the AIDS virus is a little stronger than my reluctance. I usually write in the spirit of disclosure but I want to clarify feelings and thoughts *before* my medical relationship to the AIDS crisis is established. The Health Center guarantees anonymity; even if I decide to make a secret of my lab report, it will alter the way I see myself and, doing that, alter everything. Like other gay men, to be on the safe side I behave as though I'm contagious. An HIV positive gives that proposition—with some exceptions—medical certitude, while an HTLV–3 negative puts me—with fewer exceptions—in the clear.

I read the endless AIDS coverage in the gay press. These reports cannot gauge the accumulating sorrow because no language can express so great a feeling; I get an inkling of its scale in the torrent of factual coverage, a deluge of facts, debated and repeated, as though sheer enumeration could save us. I wonder: will a cough lead to pneumocystis, headache to lesions, a mark on my skin to Kaposis? My boyfriend speculates that, like a war, the full effects of the trauma won't appear till the disease is "conquered." Sometimes, in the calmest moments, dozing, an image of myself flashes on my mind's screen: I'm sobbing deeper than I ever have, arms in the air, head thrown back theatrically, as it has never been, as I would never allow.

Immediately I have an impulse to make comparisons and draw morals, to deflect attention from the real trouble, to give a past tense to what can't be fathomed. Anxiety demands a universal to escape itself. All right: AIDS is the disease of the 80s. Why? Well, the destruction of the immune system is an allegory of the breakdown of "basic structures" now experienced by our country and the West. Or: AIDS is bad news from a remote yet governing part of the body (the immune system, the CIA) and I theorize that the virus was concocted by one of the more feverish outposts of government-sponsored research. Or: AIDS resembles radiation poisoning's silent decomposition, its scientific unwholesomeness and cataclysmic forecast for all people. Or: AIDS is the result of sexual imbalance—we were unnatural or too natural (a death's head leers from the crotch).

These interpretations are foolish and comforting, as though finding *what exists* were the same as inventing a moral, as though at some moral's bottom line I'd stop being dazed and scattered. I can't supply meaning to a catastrophe whose real life takes place in the microscopic distance (so near it's far) where viruses are normal and *my* existence is an unlikely game of creation and destruction without any stakes. I feel this chemical remoteness to be the void in its mechanical uncaring and its absolute precondition for my existence. Why ask it for comfort when it illustrates the opposite, that is, the improbability of life. I discover this solitude when I lie awake, aware of my existence, wondering if my breath is labored or shallow, if I feel exhausted or just fatigued, wondering if I should associate the operations of my body, the deep hum or tension that is myself, with the workings of the virus.

AIDS must be seen as this rent in the fabric of life, personal and public. Like other catastrophes, AIDS heightens our lives in a way that we would never want. I'm cast into the region of the uncanny where animate and inanimate blur. I tell myself, I can't die this way, but of course I can. A sense of destiny asserts itself in the face of so many blighted ones—the "me" avid to continue being me comes forward.

With that in mind, can I manufacture some historical perspective? During the late sixties I, and others, glimpsed Utopia for a moment. We saw that the world was the world, not someone's interpretation of it; that life was the fulfillment of itself; that our destinies—our selves—were our own. This revolutionary idea appeared at once on different fronts, and American identity revamped itself. Actually, we merely claimed the happiness and freedom that were promised to us throughout our childhoods in the deceptive fifties. For me, a budding gay man, the new identity meant sexuality. The rules an invisible world made for me had become opaque; I could see they were obviously invented for someone else's benefit at the price of my own emptiness; they seemed to disappear in a burst of laughter. First, we created a mental and geographical terrain in which we could know each other and be known, could recognize gestures and share meaning; second, our sexuality provided a sublime to transcend and dissolve those new-found selves.

In short, it was gay community—well organized, inventive, imperfect, equipped for the seventies and eighties, that is, for urban life, and subject to its pluses and minuses. Unlike older communities, it thrived in an urban setting, in commercial institutions like bars and baths and cafes; it added its own chapter to the history of love in those decades. What other population could respond to urban anonymity by incorporating it into the group's lovelife as anonymous sex? To the degree that my own aroused body expressed the sublime, it broke every social contract, while the invitation to the sexual act unified a community and was its main source of communication, validating other forms of discourse. A gay cookbook? Put a naked chef on the cover. The task of being the American libido more or less passed from Blacks to gay men. Gay Christmas?—naked Santa. As we created the community it taught us a new version of who we were, then we became it. This shift in perception about oneself is almost mystical, with the implied reordering of priorities.

Inevitably, a reaction. A new model showed us that the sexuality we had thought *we* discovered was actually a 20th-century invention, part of an ongoing specialization process—as specialized, in fact, as the 20th-century version of heterosexuality. Science and authority shape these identities as much as we. Moreover, the sexual revolution peaked and declined well before the onset of AIDS. Finally, identity and consumerism share an equal sign more than ever before—urgent greed, as though the American bandwagon were pulling out for good: yuppies, guppies, an impoverishment of life for which we feel rightly ashamed. Gay community incorporates commodity life into its dynamic, as it did anonymity. Still, where are the selves we discovered, the selves that were discoverers?

It's easy to show that the world is distant, life is distant, we have the vocabulary for that: disjunction and pastiche. (Retro-modes inform architecture, fashion, politics—let's get *back* to America. The big movies are wry reworkings of the old genres.) But a touch is itself, a meeting place for the body and the sublime; it disregards language which wants to generalize, negotiate. This unique "meeting place" also describes death (if anything does). That's why observance both of sex and death can function as a community sublime. To make death general, to say ten thousand died of AIDS, is an example of how language lies. Each death is beyond language.

And yet: ten thousand have died, more on the way. I imagine—with inescapable racism and also because it's true—epidemics always happening in the Third World. Our last scourge was the Spanish flu in 1918–19, which killed 500,000—but doesn't the past in this respect resemble a Third World country? Now gays bear the contempt that the U.S.A. has for anyone in trouble. Reagan won't associate himself with homosexuality or a disease. It's a public impulse to silence that affects everyone. I'm still a little shocked when I see the word homosexual in the papers, let alone AIDS; and how confusing to associate the national libido with death.

"Ten thousand have died"—an example of how language lies in articulation and Reagan lies in silence. In bed, when I listen to my body for distant alarms, I am in a time and class by myself. Still, AIDS creates such magnitude of *loss* that now death is where gay men experience life most keenly as a group. It's where we learn about love, where we discover new values and qualities in ourselves. Death joins if not replaces sex as the community sublime. We used to have the baths, now we have the Shanti Project and other volunteer organizations that institutionalize the approach of death, and AIDS support groups, and safe sex clubs where sexuality is framed by the AIDS crisis. A sex-slave auction benefit for the Shanti Project certainly deserves its own exegesis under the heading Mix-and-Match—and there's telephone sex, changes in sex practices even between longtime lovers (sex acts also have a history), the innumerable AIDS journals and recountings. I read the obituaries in the gay newspapers instead of the sex ads. Stories about AIDS patients and treatments are passed around, traded, repeated; they help me in my solitude; they are the very matter that creates community, gives it its character, its form and being.

But everything disperses before the question, will I die soon? For that reason it's an unfair question, it breaks the social contract—and it's the only sensible question to ask. What other purpose does the mind have, if not to navigate the body safely through life? Back to the Health Center: a taste of adrenaline thins my saliva. My heart beats; I flip magazine pages; a nurse calls my number; she finds a vein; it fills a test tube. I always feel self-love whenever my blood appears, in a vial or as a taste in my mouth or when it surfaces through a cut or a puncture. These days my blood is an impressive and dangerous substance. It stands alone now, at attention in its test tube like a Messenger from the *Egyptian Book of the Dead.* It's hard to remain clear when a jackal-headed scientist weighs my heart against a white feather. In two weeks I will learn the results. I hope I can get out of this alive, the mind says, referring to life and not *able to* imagine alternatives.

* * *

I wrote "HIV" in 1986; in 1988 I want to add: 1. AIDS has been diagnosed in about 59,000 Americans, of whom about 33,000 have died. 2. First steps towards treatment now exist. People who died two years ago might be alive if AZT or AL721 arrived sooner, and I am haunted by friends who had nothing to stop their fall. The politics of treatment and research is radicalizing a generation—demonstrations, sit-ins, civil disobedience. AIDS politics is complex, but not too complex to have shining heroes like ACT UP (New York) and "AIDS Treatment News" (San Francisco), and villains like the NIH and the FDA, erratic and secretive agencies who support the pharmaceutical industry over the health of people with AIDS. 3. In the U.S. any publicity is good publicity; AIDS put homosexuals on the map. Gays have gone from national invisibility to the front page, generating interest if not enthusiasm. *Time* magazine *apologized* for not covering the March on Washington. Our protests have become American history: the Smithsonian collects AIDS posters, pamphlets, ephemera. A profound shift is occurring in our image. For the first time we are widely portrayed. 4. I am more afraid of AIDS because I see the example of so many deaths, and less afraid because of treatment and the "companionship" of so many normalizing factors, articulations, groups, and institutions. AIDS has become a kind of career; diagnosis means work and struggle, a more perilous future.

ROBERT GLÜCK

About AIDS: there are hidden and unsung victims. They are the chimpanzees that are bred for research and used in captivity, isolation, and suffering for the purpose of AIDS research, among others. These animals do not contract the disease naturally. They are entered rectally, lesions are created in their colons, and the virus is inserted up their anus, in the hope that it will "take."

Much of research dollars are funnelled into this freakish and useless activity. Much can be learned with the unfortunate humans who have AIDS. Much more can be studied with cell cultures. But we continue to exploit and torture the higher primates, our brothers and sisters, as well as billions of other mammals in lucrative and immoral experimentation.

RACHEL ROSENTHAL

For Bill Schwedler

He gave the best parties, big dancing parties, and whenever I drink rum or look at Roseville, which he collected, I think of him. He wore electric blue and green contact lenses at the same time and these colors, maybe his favorites, were also in his large abstract paintings which were kind of like aerial maps, as if he were letting you know there was a way to get to know him or to get to him. When he got sick, around 1980, he was rushed to the hospital. Maybe it was something he got in Mexico. Maybe it was parasites in the brain. Samples of his blood were sent to Atlanta and no one knew what it was. He went into and out of comas. His best friend passed the better part of a year in hospitals with him, not knowing what was happening to Bill or why. Bill never knew what hit him.

Then, a little later, what Bill died of was given a name. *The New York Post* screamed headlines and attacked gay men, the gay "lifestyle," as carriers of a specifically gay disease—the gay cancer. Against a social wallpaper patterned of ignorance and irrationality, young men, acquaintances, friends, or friends of friends, suddenly got sick. A woman friend told me that one day, three years ago, she was in her local cheese and bread store. She touched a loaf of bread and the owner yelled hysterically, "Don't touch that. AIDS." She said to him and the crowd in the store. "This is not the way you get AIDS. You shouldn't say things like that." And she walked out.

The gay community rallied itself, began to and continues to teach all of us how to fight back and defend against outrageous offenses—prejudice and indifference. Other discriminated-against minorities—Hispanics, Blacks, and IV drug users—have organized to alert their communities. And in many ways the fight has just begun. For me, a heterosexual white feminist, I'm concerned, involved, not simply because heterosexuals are and will be affected, but because, apart from the tragedy of illness and lost life, homophobia is a form of sexism, virulent in its consequences.

Ultimately AIDS will test all of us: to react without hysteria, to react against unreason with reason, to find ourselves in "others," especially when we discover in ourselves fears and denials we didn't know we had, to find strength when we didn't know or think we'd need it. I'm hoping that those of us writers and artists fortunate enough to be well and alive, for however long, will think about the time we're in, not just get used to it, figure out something to say about it, a way to live and work being conscious of it, not raise the rhetoric or use the disease for its metaphors and potentially sensational images, and finally not just consider ourselves lucky to be okay.

LYNNE TILLMAN

Weeping Women

Weeping Women
NANCY SPERO

LEON GOLUB

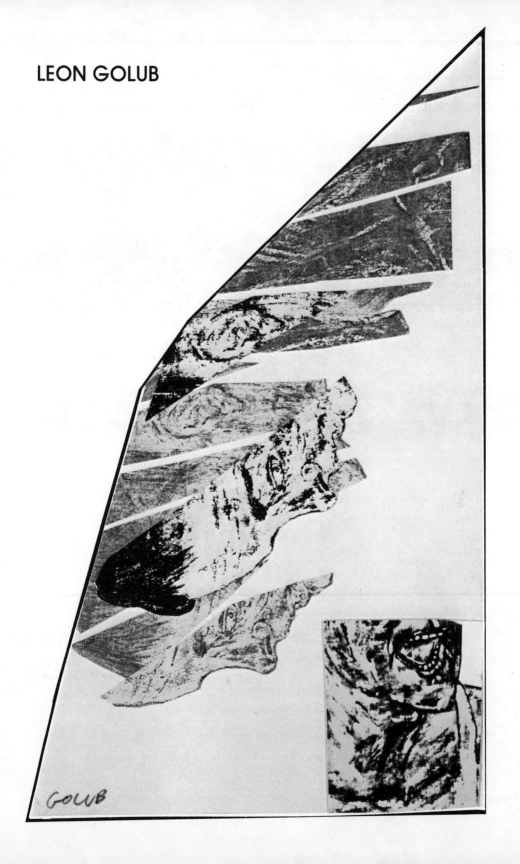

A Last Letter

"It's like war time now," my aunt told me a few weeks ago. She lived in France during World War II. "You young people are losing friends and relatives just as if it were bullets taking them away."

She's right, it's a war zone, but it's a different battlefield. It's not bullets that catch these soldiers, and there's no bombs and no gunfire. These people are dying in a whisper.

In 1982 my best friend died of AIDS. Since then there have been so many more friends I've lost. We all have. Through all of this I have come to realize that the most painful tragedy concerning AIDS death has to do with something much larger than the loss of human life itself. There is a deepening horror more grand than the world is yet aware. To see it we have to watch closely who is being stolen from us. Perhaps there is no hope left for the whole of humankind, not because of the nature of the epidemic, but the nature of those it strikes.

Each friend I've lost was an extraordinary person, not just to me, but to hundreds of people who knew their work and their fight. These were the kind of people who lifted the quality of all our lives, their war was against ignorance, the bankruptcy of beauty, and the truancy of culture. They were people who hated and scorned pettiness, intolerance, bigotry, mediocrity, ugliness, and spiritual myopia; the blindness that makes life hollow and insipid was unacceptable. They tried to make us see.

All of these friends were connected to the arts. Time and history have proven that the sensitive souls among us have always been more vulnerable.

My friend Gordon Stevenson, who died in 1982, was a filmmaker. His insights turned heads. With his wife, Muriel, who starred in his low-budget films, he was on the road to a grand film future, one that would serve to inspire and influence a lot of people. When Muriel died in a car accident in Los Angeles, it wasn't long after that Gordon started getting sick.

We thought it was mourning that was wasting him, until he was eventually diagnosed and admitted to the hospital with AIDS. He demanded that I didn't visit him there, and I honored his wish, so we talked on the phone every day and he wrote me one letter.

It was written on his own paper, with his designed letterhead: a big black heart, inscribed with the words Faith, Hope, and Charity on a background of orange. It was the last letter I received from him. He died the day I got it. I still have it, it's all frayed but the message is crisp.

Dear Cookie,

Yesterday when I talked to you on the phone, I didn't know what to say. . . . Yes you're right, all of us "high riskers" have been put through an incredible ordeal—this is McCarthyism, a witch hunt, a "punishment" for being free thinkers, freedom fighters, for being "different."

I think if you told kids that measles was caused by excessive masturbation, and were made to wear T shirts to school that said "contaminated" so that no one would sit near them or play with them, and then put in a hospital ward with other measles patients to have swollen glands ripped out, spots cut off, radiation bombardment, and tons of poison to kill the measles, all the while their parents telling them that it serves them right, masturbation is a sin, they're gonna burn in hell, no allowance, no supper for a week, and the doctors telling them that it's the most fatal disease of the century . . . I think you could produce a large number of measles deaths.

Instead the child is kept at home, given ginger ale, jello, and chicken soup, and reassured by a loving mother, whom they trust absolutely, that it's nothing serious and will go away in a few days—and it does.

Our problem is that we are all alone in the cruelest of cruel societies with no one we love and trust absolutely.

All we really need is bread, water, love, and work that we enjoy and are good at, and an undying faith in and love of ourselves, our freedom, and our dignity. All that stuff is practically free, so how come it's so hard to get—and how come all these assholes and "professionals," friends and foes, family and complete strangers are always trying to convince us to follow their dumb rules, give up work in order to be a client of theirs, give up our freedom and dignity to increase their power and control?

I still don't want you to visit me here. I'm much worse, visually, than when you saw me last, so until I'm feeling stronger and looking better, let's leave it this way.

I hope this letter finds you in good spirits. I hope you're not upset that I don't want you to visit me. I wish you happiness, love, prosperity, and a limitless future.

I KNOW, I KNOW, I KNOW that somewhere there is paradise and although I think it's really far away, I KNOW, I KNOW, I KNOW I'm gonna get there, and when I do, you're gonna be one of the first people I'll send a postcard to with complete description of, and map for locating . . .

Courage, bread, and roses,

Gordon

COOKIE MUELLER

Undoing the Folded Lies

Months ago, crossing lower Fifth Avenue here in New York, I saw inscribed on a mailbox an equation, "Gay=AIDS=Death." Other graffiti along the avenue that late morning read, "AIDS will kill all faggots." At the corner of Fifth and 21st I looked down to see a pink triangle stenciled on the sidewalk along with the now-famous equation, "Silence=Death." Like other slogans coming out of the gay rights and AIDS movements— "Stop the lies, challenge bigotry" and "Fight AIDS, not gays"—"Silence= Death" was yet another one that rattled around inside my head signifying little more than a cliché to me. Until that afternoon on Fifth Avenue, that is, when some synapse clicked and I understood that yes, silence *is* death, that we can no longer afford the luxury of silence or politeness given the bigotry at play in this nation. In the face of all this pain that is beyond any meaning, we are obligated to rage and scream and point accusing fingers at the Dannemeyers, the Buckleys, the Buchanans, the Breslins, and the other hypocrites in this country.

These are vicious political times. At the Conservative Political Action Conference held earlier this year in Washington—and attended by the president, Lyn Nofziger, and Jack Kemp, among other luminaries—a policy analyst at the House Republican Study Group, Karen Burke, criticized federal support going to the treatment of AIDS patients and announced that within five years one-quarter to one-half of the gay population of the US would be dead. At that statement, a majority of the audience of 2,000 cheered and applauded. Vicious times indeed.

But is this any more vicious than a noted gay writer propagating the myth that one out of two gay men in the US will be dead in two years? Any more vicious than a pretty 37-year-old novelist turning on me, his lush blond hair falling to his shoulders, his tan radiant on a cold, gray April day, pointing to a poster for a benefit for the AIDS Resources Center entitled "Writers & AIDS," insisting that he resents being linked to "that disease." "Don't writers have enough difficulties without being linked to *that?*" he snarls.

And so we choose not to remain silent. We respond to the disease and the bigotry it has allowed to surface. Dancers have danced for life, musicians have played for life, singers have sung for the living, writers sit pounding out their essays, stories, novels, poems. We cannot, however much *they* want us to, go quietly from their dinner tables; we cannot remain silent for a moment.

AIDS kills people, people I've lived with, fucked with, eaten with, people who sang in cabarets, directed off-Broadway, danced at Lincoln Center, acted on Broadway, people who wrote, wrote, wrote against the madness of this dying millennium. This disease is names, names of men we have nursed, tended, loved, sobbed over. This disease is early mornings with my coffee scanning the obituary page in the *Times*, drawn to certain telling first names like Scott or Christopher or Paul or, yes, Gregory.

　　AIDS, too, is close to giving the *coup de grace* to the gay rights movement as our energies and monies go to all the AIDS organizations, with less and less understanding that the battle for civil rights cannot be suspended. Darrell Yates Rist is correct: for most of this decade we have been frantically building AIDS organizations, taking care of our own, emptying our checkbooks to support AIDS groups, volunteering our hours for people with AIDS the way we never did for our civil rights. AIDS is everything now, a death watch for our community and our rights. How can it be otherwise in these times when the head of a prominent national gay organization hails the Senate's passage of a $1 billion AIDS bill even if it contains three riders introduced by Senator Jesse Helms (R, North Carolina) that only hasten our demise—including a prohibition on any public funding going to federal programs that directly or indirectly condone homosexual behavior. And we applaud this bill as a great victory? We've been sold out by ourselves, by our complacency, by a leadership that only wants to be at the right dinner parties on the fabled Upper East Side. No, we mustn't offend our hosts by talking about our legal right to exist, about institutionalized homophobia, about fag bashing, about racism in our community. We think we've arrived politically, but as our leadership cheers this AIDS bill, we find we're really arriving in the camps in which Congressman Dannemeyer (R, California) would have us quarantined.

　　And so, as a private person, I sit here and weep with the news that arrives weekly of another acquaintance euphemistically "diagnosed" or another friend hospitalized or dead. And as a public person I rage against the disease and the vicious hatred that the presence of this virus has unleashed in this country. And I write—we write—faster and faster now on these PCs, trying to say all that we must before we lose our voices. Like Auden, "All I have is a voice/to undo the folded lie."

GREGORY KOLOVAKOS

Paris with Johnny

I always thought that when I'd go
to Paris Johnny would be there to
welcome me.
I thought this as we entered the
city by car. The trip suddenly
felt lonely without his presence.
From the European auto the
French excitement depressed
me. All I wanted was my Johnny-friend
back.
A shrill of electricity went up my
spine.
A pale green and blue hue was
on my right shoulder.

Outside, an old man walked in front of our moving car. His head landed on
the pavement. I saw his head, under the car, at the wheel, there was no time
to stop from running over an old Parisian man by some stupid American
artists who think they know everything.

We got out of the car. The man stood up. The car ran over him but he was
not hurt. The car ran over his head with the tire track still on his beret. You
don't question luck, happiness and health. You don't question an angel in
Paris.

When I sat in the car I knew it was Johnny. I could hear him chuckling. I
could hear him speak about the Pompidou, Marie Antoinette and cham-
pagne. It was the color of cactus, the color of moss, the color of everlasting.
And I tried to smell his breath. Then I cried. My friend had died of modern
plague and I felt so guilty.

Cause I hadn't died with him.
I felt guilty cause I wasn't sick.
All of my friends were dying on me.
I hate the people I love now.

I told him I hated his father for not announcing his death. And
Johnny-spirit said "How could he? He never announced my life."

And I asked him if he had seen Baby Girl Corey
who had died in the same way?
Had he seen her in the wind?
"No, I've seen her in the stars."

And I told My Johnny-heart how I hated his father
for never accepting his sexual preference.
And Johnny-Love just sang:
"My spirit is stronger than my flesh.
  My soul is larger than my body.
  Don't worry, I visit the provider
                        the punisher
                        the moneyman.
  I am sleepless nights.
  I am actors in dreams.
  I am conscience.

KAREN FINLEY

A share of income from sales of *City Lights Review* will be donated to
Project Open Hand, a meal service for people with AIDS and ARC.

Diane di Prima

POEMS

PARTHENOS

the black stone shines tho its
color / clarity   we cannot
do not   name   & the door
swings soundless   hingeless as the
panel in his skull
                   who enclosed
claimed the war goddess
                            she who was
Owl in Africk   before
Zeus came out of the ground

The black   stone
                  whose
clearness /   we dare not
enter   emits   a light
& the door swings   soundless
inviting   *its* light
is golden
            we know this tho the stone remains
inscrutable &

soft as the stone in
                 toad's head
Hekat
      frog-goddess   in what
was later
            Zulu

She who heals   thru darkness.

He enclosed   Durga, armed
maiden,   cast her forth   his
headache   whose armies march
chthonic   whose destruction

takes place under ground
              & she rose
feathers on her shoulders, a shadow
long as the road:
          "Athena.   New beginnings."

Now death is in the light
              it is
the light   golden   the door
soundless   the path   a silhouette
or outline of the Bird
the Owl, Hawk   all those
whose beak curves downward

Storms are bred underground   the sky
Revealer,   the
Interpreter   of what moves
in the earth.   Our dead
in the light of day
              primary
lyke   before the sun
              is created
rises   our Dead disperse
on the wind
          as   the   hairs
of her feathers   move

her feathered shield.

First light is lightning   "worms"
dart thru the void   the arrows
before the storm
              we aver / the Raveler
whose helmet
              crests in plumes
a black wind
            flows out of them
brings pestilence
             the light
at her back
           the male-born
woman,   outlined
           black   definite
the path   she sd   is the body
of the god
          / dess

```
            The death
she carries   golden   suffused
inviting   —   her field is the
entrance point     the door
emits a mist
              miasm

pharmakos
            is the stone       it glints
green   /   golden   /   black
Her feathered skull       Athena
New
     Beginnings.
```

THE SECOND DAUGHTER:
LI (BRIGHTNESS)

(for Dominique)

You enter power, but I am here before you
standing in what's left of grace on this planet
the bits shored up, to form a circle of light
I cannot abdicate, even for you
            come, join us!

You enter womanhood, I am a woman
to greet you, invest you, praise you
(there are oils for your skin, your hair)
I have not grown old suddenly before yr eyes
        have not the courtesy to be decrepit
            small
        in the wind at my back & yrs
I have dances still to dance—do you dance?
        how the lights
        dance in you, eyes & skin
                & brights of yr hair
How yr anger dances!

See how my skin
        like yrs
                takes on its sheen

after lovemaking
see how we glow!

The circle which is a spiral
stretches out
to the star of Isis
it is the stair of Light
in the upper parts glow
the Grandmothers
laughing
The Ancestress reaches her hand
to draw us up.
She is white vulture
w/ spiral neck

These years are the windings
of Light
our flesh flickers & changes
like flame.
Like flame, it holds us fast.

Luna Nueva

LUCIA BERLIN

The sun set with a hiss as the wave hit the beach. The woman continued up the checkered black and gold tiles of the malecón to the cliffs on the hill. Other people resumed walking too once the sun had set, like spectators leaving a play. It isn't just the beauty of the tropical sunset she thought, the importance of it. In Oakland the sun set into the Pacific each evening and it was the end of another day. When you travel you step back from your own days, from the fragmented imperfect linearity of your time. As when reading a novel, the events and people become allegorical and eternal. The boy whistles on a wall in Mexico. Tess leans her head against a cow. They will keep doing that forever; the sun will just keep on falling into the sea.

She walked onto a platform above the cliffs. The magenta sky reflected iridescent in the water. Below the cliffs a vast swimming pool had been built of stones into the jagged rock. Waves shattered against the far walls and spilled into the pool, scattering crabs. A few boys swam in the deeper water, but most people waded or sat on the mossy rocks.

The woman climbed down the rocks to the water. She took off the shift covering her bathing suit and sat on the slippery wall with the others. They watched as the sky faded and a new orange moon appeared in the mauve sky. *La luna!* people cried. *Luna nueva!* The evening grew dark and the orange moon turned to gold. The foam cascading into the pool was a sharp metallic white: the clothes of the bathers flowered eerie white as if under a strobe light.

Most of the bathers in the silver pool were fully clothed. Many of them had come from the mountains or ranchos far away; their baskets lay in piles on the rocks.

And they couldn't swim, so it was nice to lay suspended in the pool, for the waves to rock them and swirl them back and forth. When the breakers covered the wall it didn't seem that they were in a pool at all, but in their own calm eddy in the middle of the ocean.

Street lights came on above them against the palms on the malecón. The lights glowed like amber lanterns on their intricate wrought-iron poles. The water in the pool reflected the lights over and over, and then into dazzling fragments, then whole again like full moons under the tiny moon in the sky.

The woman dove into the water. The air was cool, the water warm and salty. Crabs raced over her feet, the stones underfoot were velvety and jagged. She remembered only then being in that pool many years ago, before her children could swim. A sharp memory of her husband's eyes looking at her across the pool. He held one of their sons as she swam with the other in her arms. No pain accompanied the sweetness of this recollection. No loss or regret or foretaste of death. Gabriel's eyes. Her sons' laughter, echoing from the cliffs into the water.

The bathers' voices ricocheted too from the stone. Ah! they cried, as at fireworks, when the young boys dove into the water. They swayed in their white clothes. It was festive, with the clothes swirling, as if they were waltzing at a ball. Beneath them, the sea made delicate traceries on the sand. A young couple knelt in the water. They didn't touch, but were so in love it seemed to the woman that tiny darts and arrows shot out into the water from them, like fireflies or phosphorescent fish. They wore white clothes, but seemed naked against the dark sky. Their clothes clung to their black bodies, to his strong shoulders and loins, her breasts and belly. When the waves ebbed out, her long hair floated up and covered them in tendrils of black fog and then subsided black and inky into the water.

A man wearing a straw hat asked the woman if she would take his babies out into the water. He handed her the smallest one, who was frightened. It slipped up through the woman's arms like a skittish baboon and climbed onto her head, tearing at her hair, coiling its legs and tail around her neck. She untangled herself from the screaming baby. Take the other one, the tame one, the man said, and that child did lie placidly while she swam with it in the water. So quiet she thought it must be asleep, but no it was humming. Other people sang and hummed in the cool night. The sliver of moon turned white like the foam as more people came down the stairs into the water. After awhile the man took the baby from her and left then, with his children.

On the rocks a girl tried to coax her grandmother into the pool. No! No! I'll fall! Come in, the woman said, I'll take you swimming all around the pool.

"You see I broke my leg and I'm afraid I'll break it again."

"When did it happen?" the woman asked.

"Ten years ago. It was a terrible time. I couldn't chop firewood. I couldn't work in the fields. We had no food."

"Come in. I'll be careful of your leg."

At last, the old lady let her lift her down from the rock and into the water. She laughed, clasping her frail arms around the woman's neck. She was light, like a bag of shells. Her hair smelled of charcoal fires. *Qué maravilla!* she whispered into the woman's throat. Her silver braid wafted out behind them in the water.

She was 78 and had never seen the ocean before. She lived on a rancho near Chalchihuitles. She had ridden on the back of a truck to the sea port with her granddaughter.

"My husband died last month."

"Lo siento."

She swam with the old lady to the far wall where the cool waves spilled over them.

"God finally took him, finally answered my prayers. Eight years he lay in bed. Eight years he couldn't talk, couldn't get up or feed himself. Lay like a baby. I would ache from being tired, my eyes would burn. At last, when I thought he was asleep I would try to steal away. He would whisper my name, a horrid croaking sound. *Consuelo! Consuelo!* and his skeleton hands, dead lizard hands would claw out to me. It was a terrible, terrible time.

"Lo siento," the woman said again.

"Eight years. I could go nowhere. Not even to the corner. *Ni hasta la esquina!* Every night I prayed to the Virgin to take him, to give me some time, some days without him."

The woman clasped the old lady and swam out again into the pool, holding the frail body close to her.

"My mother died only six months ago. It was the same for me. A terrible, terrible time. I was tied to her day and night. She didn't know me and said ugly things to me, year after year, clawing at me."

Why am I telling this old lady such a lie? she wondered. But it wasn't such a lie, the bloody grasp.

"They're gone now," Consuelo said, "We are liberated."

The woman laughed; liberated was such an American word. The old lady thought she laughed because she was happy. She hugged the woman tightly and kissed her cheek. She had no teeth so the kiss was soft as mangos.

"The Virgin answered my prayers!" she said, "It pleases God, to see that you and I are free."

Back and forth the two women flowed in the dark water, the clothes of the bathers swirling around them like a ballet. Near them the young couple kissed, and for a moment there was a sprinkle of stars overhead, then a mist covered them and the moon and dimmed the opal lamplight from the street.

"Vamos a comer, abuelita!" the granddaughter called. She shivered, her dress dripping on the stones. A man lifted the old woman from the water, carried her up the winding rocks to the malecón. Mariachis played, far away.

"Adiós!" The old woman waved from the parapet.

"Adiós!"

The woman waved back. She floated at the far edge in the silken warm water. The breeze was inexpressibly gentle.

SOUVENIRS

JAMES PURDY

A lonesome house on the outskirts of a Missouri town. IDA KEMBLE is seated in a large easy chair sewing diligently. She is about forty, but perhaps much younger. The cares of the world have descended on her. She sews incessantly as a spider spins, though she has earned enough money from making dresses for wealthy people not to have to toil so assiduously.

In the last few years she has fallen into the habit of talking to herself. The room is huge, with fifteen-foot ceilings, but few chairs and tables. A dummy for fitting clothes is at stage right.

IDA: That's that someone again out there. Sneaks up to my door, raps, and then runs off like a sneak thief. (*Calls*) Come on in why don't you. The door ain't locked. As I told Nettie the other day, if they wants to kill me they can. (*Pointing with her free hand*) It's all here, what I've earned. (*Imitating her rich customers*) What I've accrued! I tell you what. Them rich women don't know what's quality anymore. When my Mother and Grandma sewed them rich women knowed. My Mama knowed everything. Oh she could put me to shame as a seamstress. It takes the zeal out of you when you work so hard and your customer don't know velvet from pongee or silk from burlap. Everybody looks like they was wearing corn shocks. What would Mama say today if she could see the way the world has run down. I tell you when she died it was the biggest grief. I didn't realize how I depended on Mama for everything. I tell you if the continents had all divided up into little islets with the ocean roaring in between I could not have felt more lost. Without her and her guiding hand, let me tell you! (*She puts down her sewing*) I have been one lost little girl ever since. I sew so I won't notice how lost I be. Lost, lost. I was only happy when I was a girl with Mama. . . . Who are you? (*Screaming to the person she hears outside*) Damn it all. . . . I shouldn't swear. Mama was so lovely. She was lighter skinned than me. They said as a girl she passed. I get my complexion from my Daddy. He was a middleweight boxer, gone all the time. Then one day he was gone for good. Never showed up again. Mama and me went on with our sewin'. I love a steady faithful daughter, she said just before she died. You will always keep a roof over your head angel, even if you don't come into possession of a gold mine. You taught me everything, Mama. And

Grandma too. Grandma was stern though. She had two gold rings on her fingers. One for husband number one, Beauchamp Ferris, and ring number two for Jonas Cransome, that was my Granddaddy. (*Someone knocks now. . . . Calling*) I tole you the door was open. I leave it open day and night. I'm protected. I know there's a kind of angel in this old house. Tell you what, once I had a bad fever during the February thaw when the snow was so bad underfoot. I got up in the night to get some cherry wine to ease the pain and at the foot of my bed, I seen something. I don't believe in ghosts. Our church taught there wasn't none. But he was standing there looking at me and his wings moved like a young bird's. His face was golden spotted and bright over his blackness and his eyes was blue turning to sort of dark gray. He opened his mouth. I said Don't scare me, please please don't. His wings moved again and then he weren't there. I knowed then this house was protected. I wouldn't use a key *no how* on account of my visit from the angel. I wonder what he wanted. Oh how I wonder. Never did come again, but sometimes in the very still of winter, I think I hear his wings so soft moving like they would put you to sleep. Soft angel wings movin'. . . . (*The door opens slowly. She stops*) Christ in Heaven! Oh Lord! (*A young black man enters, dressed as if for a wedding ceremony. He carries a bouquet of roses. . . . Naming him*) Firmin Orenson! Where in the creation. . . .

FIRMIN: Ha. Thought I was dead didn't you. Don't deny it. Don't you deny it. You thought I was dead. Well, I'm just as real as these flowers.

IDA: (*Accepting the bouquet*) I never knowed you to care about flowers, Firmin. And I didn't think you was dead. Never so much as crossed my mind. (*Rises, and goes to the back of the stage and gets a vase with water, returns. While she was busy* FIRMIN *has been looking around the room*) Roses in February! You always did unexpected things, Firmin. (*Thinking*) You didn't steal them from somewhere, did you?

FIRMIN: (*Looking around*) Ida, don't you feel lost in so big a room? I mean. . . .

IDA: (*Sitting back sewing again*) What do you mean?

FIRMIN: It's too big for a woman all alone.

IDA: I ain't alone.

FIRMIN: You didn't get married again?

IDA: Ha! Do you think I'm crazy. Wasn't three times enough, three no-account husbands!

FIRMIN: Then you are all by yourself?

IDA: (*Nods*) I don't feel alone though. No, I ain't livin' with nobody. . . . (*Anguished*) Firmin, where you been so long?

FIRMIN: (*Sitting down slowly, gracefully, spitting on his shoes to polish them*) I been . . . just about everywhere. Oh it makes me tired to think of all the places I been.

IDA: It makes me tired just to think of you bein' tired.

FIRMIN: What do you mean by that?

IDA: 'Cause you was always such a rover. You've done everything. Everything. That's why it makes me tired, while I've just sat here through time in this room that was Mama's and Grandma's. Why sometimes I think I ain't never been out of this house in all my life.

FIRMIN: I even learned foreign languages, can you beat that?

IDA: You was always a smart boy. (*Stern*) Firmin, why have you come back when the trouble here ain't died down about you?

FIRMIN: (*Sleepily*) Nobody would know me with these clothes now, would they?

IDA: And carryin' a bouquet of roses. I s'pect not.

FIRMIN: I've changed. And I'm tired.

IDA: Firmin Orenson tired. Then the tides is tired of risin' and the wind howlin'.

FIRMIN: True, I ain't dead tired. I ain't an old man.

IDA: (*Poking fun*) No you ain't old-old, true.

FIRMIN: I wanted to see a familiar face, and hear a lullaby talk.

IDA: Lullaby, my eyes! I ain't takin' you back, you know that. I'm done with husbands.

FIRMIN: I didn't return to be took back. (*Angry*) Why can't you take what people has to give. You're proud. You're proud. That's why you're alone. You always felt you was better than the rest of us.

IDA: Not better. Just steadier.

FIRMIN: Well I've been steady in seein' everything. Whilst you has sat here like a spider spinnin' away. I been steady in never stayin' in one spot twice. And it has got into my bones. I tell you!

IDA: I has some of that light rum you was always so fond of. (*She says this worriedly*).

FIRMIN: Light rum. Where did you get that?

IDA: It was queer. A kind of peddlar comes around here, and usually he only sells me coffee beans and rice. But the other night he said, Ida Kemble, I have some very fine Caribbean light rum tonight, but I don't want no money for it from you. It's a souvenir for you.

FIRMIN: A souvenir?

IDA: (*Thinking*) A souvenir, he says, 'cause you've been so steady like your Mama and your Grandma was before you.

FIRMIN: I ain't sure what a souvenir is, Ida.

IDA: With all your travelin' around the world you don't know what a souvenir is? Poor Firmin, you. Well when you taste it maybe you'll know.

FIRMIN: I ain't got no doubt I will. (IDA *rises, goes back to the same part of the room where she drew water for the flowers, and fixes him some rum*) I ain't drinkin' alone now Ida. If you don't drink alongside o' me I will say no. Souvenir or no souvenir.

IDA: All right. It's a homecomin', and I'll join you this once. But you got to remember us Kembles is down on liquor on account of what it did to Daddy.

FIRMIN: (*Taking the drink from* IDA) Yea, I wonder what you'd do if you ever let go, sweetheart. I mean, if you just sort of billowed out. If you didn't sit here like a spider and spin, and if you just let go. If you *gathered up* life.

IDA: Don't you talk that way.

FIRMIN: (*Tasting*) Some souvenir, all right. If that's souvenir I want a whole cellar of it. Whew. That is the nectar of the gods as they say.

IDA: You didn't get nothin' that good in your travels?

FIRMIN: No siree, no ma-am no. Oh joy. So that's souvenir.

IDA: Firmin, you worry me.

FIRMIN: (*Bracing up*) There ain't no reason to worry about me.

IDA: Oh I do. I do.

FIRMIN: Don't I look good.

IDA: You look too good. Too good. I'd not have recognized you, and with the roses and all. You look like a preacher.

FIRMIN: I tell you somethin'. No maybe I won't tell you nothin'.

IDA: Firmin, did you kill those two white men like the St. Louis papers said? (FIRMIN *drinks*) You don't have to tell me if you don't want to.

FIRMIN: You know I have been made to feel guilty about so many deeds I never committed since a boy . . . I was taught to carry the burden of bad deeds from the time I quit nursing my Mama. I been carryin' so many other people's sins and deeds, how do I know now if I killed them or not. I may have killed them, I may have not. But in any case they would make me feel I was guilty of havin' done it whether I did or not.

IDA: (*Stops sewing*) Good God, how you don't level with me. Did you or didn't you? I know how you feel. But did you kill them?

FIRMIN: (*Putting down his drink and rising as if seeing into past time*) I killed them again and again. I killed them with a gun, with a knife, with an axe, with my eyes.

IDA: With your eyes?

FIRMIN: (*Turning to her*) It was my eyes that done killed them, for their wounds was not mortal. I looked at them and they said, Don't do no more, don't do no more, all the while not takin' my eyes from theirs. And the one who was dyin' said, what does that look mean, you black jigaboo motherfucker? Yes, says the other who was not all that bad wounded, What do you mean staring at us like a lunatic escaped from bolts and bars?

IDA: (*With horror*) And your reply?

FIRMIN: (*Coming out of his trance*) Oh yes, my reply. . . . I have forgot.

IDA: Forgot! When you done killed them.

FIRMIN: It was kill or be killed.

IDA: And you killed them with your eyes! (*Laughs*) I can believe it. When we was married and you looked at me sometimes—blue eyes in a black face—I felt my hour had come.

FIRMIN: (*Remembering*) I said to the two dyin' men, Ida, I said, I ain't lookin' at two white men at all. I am lookin' at God who brought me into this world to bleed and cough out my guts, and crawl on busted glass bottles and nails, while his Son only hung on that piece of cross for a couple days. I am lookin' at God, you white motherfuckers, I ain't lookin' at you. So die, while dyin' is easy. Die, die. . . .

IDA: (*Warning*) Firmin! Firmin.

FIRMIN: Yea, Firmin. You has somethin' here that belongs to me, Ida.

IDA: I s'pect so.

FIRMIN: You know so, and I hope you ain't gone and give it away.

IDA: You'll have to tell me what it is. I ain't no mind reader or gypsy fortune teller.

FIRMIN: Once when I brought you a lot of money. . . .

IDA: So you did.

FIRMIN: I put all the money on that table over there. (*Points a long time*) And you said. . . .

IDA: I remember.

FIRMIN: (*Masterful*) You said, I never seen so much money before and in gold at that.

IDA: I recall it.

FIRMIN: If you didn't I would give you one of my looks.

IDA: Don't talk to me like that.

FIRMIN: I said, With this money, Ida Kemble, I want you to make me a cloak and a hat, and supply me with a gold-headed walkin' stick that is like a scepter, I want to have the clothes of the King of Haiti, Henri Christophe. . . . Where is my cloak, Ida, for I done paid you a fortune for it?

IDA: Your cloak. Jesus oh Christ!

FIRMIN: (*Rising*) You don't have it? Or you lied and didn't make it.

IDA: (*Threatening*) I made it and I have it. Locked away.

FIRMIN: Then you go where it is locked away and produce it . . . for I be in a hurry.

IDA: Don't you issue no orders to me.

FIRMIN: I paid you in blood money.

IDA: I thought as much.

FIRMIN: But it was my blood. Sometimes you don't act like a nigger, and then I could kill you. Whenever blood is shed it is our blood, *my* blood is shed, not white folks. If I killed a million of them it would be my blood still bein' shed. It's our blood always that's shed, runnin' like water to the sea.

IDA: Firmin, you're lookin' at me that way.

FIRMIN: Where is it locked up. My cloak and diadem?

IDA: What's a diadem?

FIRMIN: A crown, Ida. A crown. My crown. Now you rise up and fetch them. 'Cause I'm not leavin' without them.

IDA: Where are you goin' after you took the risk and trouble to get here. Huh?

FIRMIN: You better go get my cloak. You was paid enough to make a thousand cloaks.

IDA: And you bccn gone ten years!

FIRMIN: Eleven!

IDA: And you killed 'em? The two white men in St. Louis?

FIRMIN: That's what the papers said.

IDA: (*Getting up*) Why couldn't you have behaved and stayed with me when I loved you best. When I needed you so after Mama went. Why couldn't my love have been enough for you. Oh, Firmin. (*He rises and takes her in his arms*)

FIRMIN: There, there. It's too late to go back. It's too late to mend what can't be mended. Go get my cloak now. Go on. I won't look at you with my terrible eyes if you be good.

IDA: I wouldn't care if you killed me too, for I'm dead anyhow . . . a dead spider spinnin'. When you went out and killed and left me, I turned into a spider spinnin'. Spinnin' spinnin', dead.

FIRMIN: Go on now. The cloak. (IDA *exits at stage left*. FIRMIN, *alone, drinks a lot of the light rum*) She don't know what I mean. She don't know when white men die it's still my blood that is shed. She don't know. 'Cause she's turned to stone, that's what. She won't feel any more. She felt too much she said once. So she won't feel. She's a spider spinnin' so she won't remember. She don't know my blood is shed every hour, minute, second. She don't see how I bleed. She fears the cruddy white people. She don't love my blood enough. That's why I left her. She don't love my blood when it is spilled. She thinks I'm guilty. Guilty of what? Guilty of bleedin'. That's what she don't understand, curse her. Thunderbolts, hit her! She wasn't up to my love. Not up to my love. (*Drinks*)

IDA: (*Enters with the sumptuous cloak of King Christophe of Haiti and the diadem*) Here, you see, I've kept it against moths and dust. It's practically new.

FIRMIN: (*Overcome by the beauty of the cloak*) Oh Christ alive. You done it. You kept it. You made it. . . . All for me. Say it was all for me.

IDA: All for you, beloved.

FIRMIN: Put me in it. (*He slowly takes off his jacket and tie and shirt and is bare chested*)

IDA: All right. (*She puts the cloak around him*)

FIRMIN: (*Exulting in the beauty of his cloak*) Oh how happy I am. And the crown.

IDA: Here, here. Let me put it on right. (*She puts the crown on him*) Oh, are you handsome. Yes, you were my only love. You and Mama. Oh, Firmin, why can't you stay? Why can't you be here? You could hide upstairs. The house has twenty rooms.

FIRMIN: If it had a million I couldn't hide good enough for they'd go in all million rooms, and spy me.

IDA: You'll leave me now I have you again?

FIRMIN: Yes, 'cause they'll come in any case, and take me from you. You know that. Oh, Ida, Ida.

IDA: What is it, love?

FIRMIN: *(Mimicking) Love.* Yes, I suppose. I suppose. If only you knew that whenever I kill a white man, my own blood was shed before him. My blood is shed all over the world. My blood runs like the river lookin' for the sea. My blood. . . . *(Goes toward the door)*

IDA: Firmin, you can't go now. You can't leave me. You can't.

FIRMIN: I told you even if you had a million rooms to hide in they'd find me. I can't stay. It could be your death too. I want you to live.

IDA: To live?

FIRMIN: To remember me, like this. *(He shows himself in the cloak)* Like the King of Haiti.

IDA: If you leave me this time, I will die. . . . I will die.

FIRMIN: No you won't . . . you'll spin, you'll . . . sew. *(She throws herself into his arms. They kiss long and ardently, then he leaves her embrace and goes out stage left)*

IDA: *(Rushing to the door)* No, no. . . . No. . . . No. . . . *(Comes back in, picks up the light rum drink he has left)* If it were strychnine, or wormwood, arsenic, rat poison or raw opium. . . . After tasting his kisses! After smellin' his arms and hair. To have him with me and then never to have him again! Oh no, oh no. The pain, the pain I cannot bear the. . . . They'll kill him! Kill him. They'll kill him. *(She is quiet for a while, as the room grows darker)* But he was right about the sewin'. I sew like a dead woman. A dead spider sewin' her web. To catch what? A ghost with wings perhaps. Sewin', workin' on. . . . And to think I tasted his lips, and smelled the wonderful smell of his armpits. . . . And then nothin', nothin' ever again. Sewin'. Just sewin'. It will keep me from going to the lunatic asylum. Or if I go they will let me sew there too. . . . I will taste his lips forever. I will never wash my mouth. I will taste his lips forever, and feel his white teeth on my mouth, his soft sweet spit like cherry wine.

CURTAIN

FEDERICO GARCIA LORCA

BUSTER KEATON'S PROMENADE

Translated by Christopher Sawyer-Lauçanno

CAST OF CHARACTERS

Buster Keaton	An owl	An American woman
A rooster	A black man	A young woman

ROOSTER: Cockledoodledoo!

(Buster Keaton enters hand in hand with his four children.)

BUSTER KEATON: *(He takes out a wooden dagger and kills them.)* My poor children!

ROOSTER: Cockledoodledoo!

BUSTER KEATON: *(Counting the bodies on the ground)* One, two, three and four. *(He grabs a bicycle and leaves.)*

(Among old gum tires and gasoline cans a black man eats his straw hat.)

BUSTER KEATON: What a beautiful afternoon!

(A parrot flutters in the neutral sky.)

BUSTER KEATON: Such pleasure to take the air on a bicycle.

OWL: Hoo, Hoo, Hoo, Hoo.

BUSTER KEATON: The birds sing so splendidly.

OWL: Hoooooooooooo.

BUSTER KEATON: It's thrilling.

(Pause. Buster Keaton ineffably crosses the bulrushes and little field of rye. The landscape recedes behind the bicycle wheels. The bicycle has only one dimension. It can enter the books and extend itself into the bread oven. Buster Keaton's bicycle does not have a caramel saddle or sugar pedals like those that villains would want. It is just an ordinary bicycle, except for being uniquely imbued with innocence. Adam and Eve would run away frightened if they were to see a glass full of water, but would caress Keaton's bicycle.)

BUSTER KEATON: Oh love! Love!

(Buster Keaton falls to the ground. The bicycle escapes him. It runs after two giant gray butterflies, crazily flying a half millimeter off the ground.)

BUSTER KEATON: *(Getting up)* I don't want to say anything. What am I going to say?

A VOICE: Simpleton.

(He continues walking. His eyes, immense and sad like those of a beast just born, dream of irises, angels and silk sashes. Glass-bottom eyes. Eyes of a stupid child. Terribly ugly. Terribly beautiful. Eyes of an ostrich. Human eyes in the sure equilibrium of melancholy. In the distance he sees Philadelphia. Although the city's inhabitants already know that the old poem of the Singer sewing machine can encircle the grand greenhouse roses of winter, they will never be able to comprehend the subtle poetic difference existing between a cup of hot tea and a cup of cold tea. Philadelphia shines in the distance.)

BUSTER KEATON: This is a garden.

(An American woman with celluloid eyes comes through the grass.)

AMERICAN WOMAN: Good afternoon.

(Buster Keaton smiles and in a "close up" looks over the woman's shoes. Oh what shoes! We can't allow those shoes. It took three crocodile hides to make them.)

AMERICAN WOMAN: Do you have a sword adorned with myrtle leaves?

(Buster Keaton shrugs his shoulders and lifts his right foot.)

AMERICAN WOMAN: Do you have a ring with a poison stone?

(Buster Keaton slowly shuts his eyes and lifts his left foot.)

AMERICAN WOMAN: Well then?

(Four seraphim with wings of gauze celestially dance among the flowers. The young ladies of the city play the piano as if they were riding a bicycle. The waltz, the moon, and the canoes stir the precious heart of our friend. With great surprise to all, autumn has invaded the garden, like water on a lump of sugar.)

BUSTER KEATON: *(Sighing)* I would like to be a swan. But even though I would like to be, I cannot. Because . . . Where did I leave my hat? Where is my wing collar and my moiré tie? What a disgrace!

(A wasp-waisted young woman with a high bodice and stiff collar enters riding a bicycle. She has a nightingale's head.)

YOUNG WOMAN: Whom do I have the honor to greet?

BUSTER KEATON: *(Bowing)* Buster Keaton.

(The young woman faints and falls off the bicycle. Her striped legs tremble on the grass like two dying zebras. A gramophone announces a thousand shows at once: "In America there are nightingales.")

BUSTER KEATON: *(Kneeling)* Miss Eleonora. Forgive me. Miss! *(Lower)* Miss! *(Even lower)* Miss! *(He kisses her.)*

(Against the Philadelphia skyline shine the policemen's flashing stars.)

GIORGIO MANGANELLI

from

Centuria
One Hundred Little Epic Tales
Translated from the Italian by John Satriano

TWO

A gentleman of fairly good upbringing and dignified manners met, after an absence of months, owing to horrible wartime events, the woman he was in love with. He didn't kiss her, but, instead, drawing away in silence, vomited at some length. He had no intention of giving the astonished woman any explanation for vomiting like that; nor did he give one to anybody; and only patiently with time did he come to understand that that vomiting had expelled from his body all the innumerable images of the woman he loved, all the images which had been deposited in it and had amorously intoxicated it. But, at that moment, he understood that it would no longer be possible to treat that woman as if the only thing existing between them had been love, a delicate love, concerned only with overcoming every obstacle and with touching the other's skin, forever. He had experienced the toxicity of love, and understood that the toxicity of distance was the only alternative to the toxicity of intimacy, and that he had vomited out the past to make room for the vomit of the future. Although it might have been impossible to explain it to someone else, he knew the symptom of a necessary love was not sighs, but vomit, just as death is the only certain symptom of life.

From that moment, he has found himself in the delightfully tormenting situation of not being able to either disdain, or woo, or esteem, or contemplate the woman whom, without a doubt, he loves—indeed, whom he loves in an unbearable way, now that he has made her a participant in his vomiting—or keep the secret from her that he, in order to accept her totally, has to absorb her, to make her, from the very moment in which she was revealed to him as poison, what she is unaware of being, and which he has no desire to explain to her. Meanwhile, everywhere, life is becoming unstable, new wars are threatening. Death notices are being prepared, and the earth is becoming soft, in anticipation of graves. Everywhere, posters are being pasted up which explain the meaning of blood. Since no one speaks of vomit, the man in love thinks that the problem is either ignored (or given out as being ignored) or perhaps too well known. He kisses his fiancée, entrusts the wedding night to her care and, vomiting, bestraddles the powerful horse of death.

TWENTY

The lady who, dressed carefully, with reserved fantasy, trusting more to the rhythm of her body than to the polluting adornment of her clothes, that woman who is crossing the street, her gaze fixed on the number of a bus she thinks is the one she has to take, though she isn't sure, since she has quite a few stops to make, that woman is fairly young and yet I refused to ask her a single question, and therefore, in the act itself of crossing the street, with the ephemeral and neutral complicity of the traffic lights, the subtitles of her life attach themselves to her body. Perhaps you wouldn't call her a beautiful woman, inasmuch as you are sensual and ephemeral— O, loathsome traffic lights!— but you cannot help but admire the solid and at the same time watchful way with which she registers her body upon the street.

This woman has been in love with four men: and now she leads a solitary, but not abandoned, life. There are only three hundred meters left to the bus stop. She fell in love with her first man when, still a girl, she came to understand herself in conversing with a certain musician. I hesitate to call him a musician. Perhaps a genius, certainly vulgar, a trivial sort of genius. The long discussions built like great country houses quieted the way she used to laugh, they gave her mouth a more composed look. After her first possessor, she met a myopic and patient cybernetic; if the first man had been a figure hurriedly drawn on the wall, with traces of the design showing for years afterward, this one was fatuous, vile, eloquent. She lingered there out of love of eloquence. The cybernetic said, "Wait for me," and walked off down the street.

One day, two years later, while she was out looking for a zipper, she had a fling: she doesn't know whether out of love, distraction, hurry, a failure to communicate. A foreigner? She isn't sure. She had a son by him, as you can see. Next she fell madly in love with a tulip farmer, who played the lottery and believed that God had the hiccups. He looked at her son with suspicion but, oh no, without hate.

Now that the woman is dead—she already took that bus I was talking about, but now it's of no importance—she walks through the labyrinths of Sheol and tries to understand why her son, who survives her, grief-stricken and alone, on the strange curves of the earth, was born out of an affair with a man whose name she cannot remember. On account of this she has that strange, tormented and questioning face, with jutting chin, and the hint of a smile just behind her pupils.

TWENTY-ONE

Every morning, upon awakening—a reluctant awakening that could be defined as lazy—this gentleman starts his day off with a quick inventory of the world. He has realized for quite a while now that every time he wakes up, he wakes up in a different point of the cosmos, even if the earth, his place of habitation, does not appear changed in any intrinsic way. As a little boy, he had been convinced that, in its movements through space, the earth sometimes passes close to or actually into hell, while at the same time it is never allowed to pass into paradise, because such an experience would render any further continuation of the world impossible, superfluous, ridiculous. Therefore, paradise has to stay out of earth's way at all costs, in order not to harm the carefully drawn out and incomprehensible plans of creation. Even now—as an adult man, who drives his own car—something of that infantile hypothesis has stayed with him. He has somewhat laicized it now, and the question that poses itself is more metaphoric and, by all appearances, detached: he knows that, while he is sleeping, the whole world gets displaced—as happens in dreams—and that every morning the world's pieces, though more or less belonging to one part, are located in different places. He doesn't claim to know what this displacement means, but he knows that sometimes he notices the presence of abysses, the beckonings of jutting cliffs, or lengthy plains of a rare type through which he would like to roll—occasionally he thinks of himself as a round, celestial body—on and on. Sometimes he has a confused impression of grass, at others an exciting (but, not rarely, unpleasant) sensation of being illuminated by a number of different suns, not always mutually friendly. At other times, he distinctly hears a crashing of waves, which may be either a tempest or a calm; at others still, it is his own position in the world that brutally reveals itself to him: for example, when cruel and straining jaws seize him by the nape of the neck, as had to have happened time and time again to his weary ancestors, in the teeth of savage beasts, whose faces he has never seen. For some time he has been aware that one never wakes up in one's own room: he has, in fact, concluded that "room" is a thing that doesn't exist, that walls and sheets are an illusion, a kind of make-believe; he knows that he is suspended in the void, that, like everyone else, he is the center of the world, from which infinite infinities take their departure. He knows that he could not bear so much horror, and that the room, and even the abyss and the inferno, are inventions meant to protect him.

from

INDICOS PANICOS
Singing in the Desert

CRISTINA PERI ROSSI

Translated from the Spanish by Sean Higgins

Someone singing in the desert shouldn't surprise anyone, for many people have done it since the beginning of time, when everything (including the sky) was sand and the oceans were frozen.

We know that they sang in the desert, but we didn't listen to them; because of this we might be able to say that, up to a certain point, they sang for themselves, although that was not the original purpose of their song.

Given that we didn't hear them, we might also doubt that they had really sung; nevertheless, we are sure that their voices rise up or rose up over the sands of the desert, with the sort of certainty that permits us to affirm that the Earth is round, without having seen its shape, or that it whirls around the Sun; all this aside, we realize that we are moving. It's this type of conviction that makes us suppose that they had sung in the desert, in spite of our not having heard them. The reason is that song is one of the aptitudes of people, and because deserts exist.

She sings in a low voice. The sands are white, and the sky yellow. She is lightly seated on a dune, with her eyes closed; the sand covers her neck, her eyelashes, and her lips, through which pass a thin stream of sound like a liqueur over the parched Earth. Even though she sings without anyone listening to her, we are sure that she sings or that she has sung at some time.

With certainty the stream of her voice is lost almost immediately without echo or reverberation in the yellow space surrounding her. And the Sun, which sucks voraciously the few drops of water from a nearby lake, also drinks the notes of her song in a furor. Not for that would she leave off singing, nor does she raise her voice: she continues singing in the midst of the white sands, from the pyramids of salt that rise up like temples to a blind, obtuse divinity. The sands, which have devoured more than one camel and rider, subdue the notes of her song. But the next day (or the other night because we can suppose that she also sings beneath a dark sky, in the solitude of the desert) she once again raises up her voice. Such insistence does not surprise anyone, for it seems to be intrinsic to her song, and at times, intrinsic to the desert. After a certain point it would seem difficult to imagine a desert without a woman poised on a dune, singing, and without being heard.

The nature of the song is unknown to us although we are persuaded that the song exists. When she goes down to the city (because she is not always in the desert: at times she shares in the life of our cities and carries out the conventional, ordinary acts that we go on repeating from birth) we accept her as one more inhabitant, because in reality, nothing distinguishes her from ourselves, except for the fact that she sings in the desert: something that we could forget, given that nobody hears her. When she disappears again, we suppose that she has returned to the desert and that in the midst of the white sands and the frozen ocean of a sky, she raises up her voice, elevates her song that, like a drop of water fallen from space, is swallowed up by the dunes.

Janine Pommy Vega

POEMS

THE WALK

A woman, twisted at the edge of her seat,
walks into the woods
walks blindly, she intends to scream
she intends to walk to the old friend, the
hickory tree at the top of the road,
and fling her arms around him, and pound
the snow at his feet.

Instead, she walks a little farther.
She doesn't want the light across the meadow
in on her screams; the family in there, blanking
out the sound during commercials, alerted suddenly
to the wild dreams of trees.
She continues climbing, past the maple tree of a hundred
walks, her feet striding purposefully
into the dark.

The stars come suddenly to her, decorating
the arms of the forest—Orion, Sirius, Pleiades,
Hyades, Auriga, Perseus and Algol the demon star
thrust away from him
Due north due north Polaris over the brow of the hill
And she doesn't want to build another bookshelf
She doesn't want to pocket this away,
to squirrel it in some quiet corner where she will
never find it again.

She reaches the stream. It is the only darkness
in the forest, and the only time she takes out
her flashlight. Where she was stepping was indeed
a rock. What she reached for was the water.
Her hands are warm. It is an old pact
between her and the beech trees rustling on the path.

Her war is with herself, herself and containment
Not against the footsteps of a path, or the sensible
way out, but against the ironing out of wildness,
her own wildness.

Her heart is stirred as a creature under the trees
looking up at lights. No wind, the tears roll down
her face. She is safe in her love for the stars,
the water, her commitment to beauty.
Is it beauty, really? Does it matter?
She doesn't build shelves, nor bookcases, with
every book a brick one keeps for safety hidden
in the corner. Her love turns a corner,
it dips over the rise in the hill, and whoops down
the other side. Perhaps her books will be kisses,
wet leaves under the snow that show up dark
on a moonless night.

Perhaps she will never reach Jerusalem on a camel,
or see the Southern Cross again. The north woods
is where she happens to be, divining the branches before
they hit her face. Perhaps she will never build
a bookcase. Perhaps she doesn't have to.

OLD WOMAN OF AUTUMN

O pagan poet you
And I are one
In this—we lose our god
At set of sun.

Paddy Kavenaugh

Hallowe'en night. Open the window. Listen to the footsteps of
everything out there walking. The oak leaves falling. Brooms in all the
corners, the wind is sweeping. Pilgrim footsteps stitch the hills. Midway
point in the journey to the dark.

Stags pursue the oak leaves dreaming
acorns in the autumn dusk

> She stands under a dry moon turning
> hills and fields to rust.

The window opens by itself. Shine on a trumpet between the eyes. Lone star in insomniac forest. The rusty streambed sings louder than sundown in places. The wind gathers skirts of a thousand trees, covering tracks of larger things.

> Stags pursue the oak leaves dreaming
> acorns in the autumn dusk
> She walks under a dry moon turning
> forest and stream to rust.

Midway point into the dark, the hills already humming in bass note winter voice. The choir of lost things. Sun eaten by a stone mouth. Heart of sun devoured for solar plexus warmth, where the seed sleeps.

> Stags pursue the oak leaves dreaming
> acorns in the autumn dusk
> She leaps under a dry moon turning
> crevice and cliff to rust.

The hills roll away, the wind touching every ledge and rockface. A last celebration of red leaves, fires, wrinkled faces. I lift my skirts up, over the flames, to the dance of the skinny ankles.

> Stags pursue the oak leaves dreaming
> acorns in the autumn dusk
> She dances under a dry moon turning
> sun and stars to rust.

Ghost Story

LESLIE DICK

Night fell.

She said: Paper dolls can't sit down; they're inflexible, flat like a picture. You're just meant to dress them and undress them, you can make them talk but their clothes tend to fall off, those white flaps never hold the dress on if you make a paper doll do anything at all except stand there. For Christmas I got a Jackie Kennedy paper doll, and her wardrobe included the very same pale pink Chanel suit she was wearing on that fateful day in Dallas when the president was shot. There was even the pillbox hat, a little square of pink paper, with a slit in it, to slip over her black cardboard hair. She was smiling, that big smile, and her black hair curled around her face. One arm was part of the body, and one stretched out, so you could hang her handbag on it. Her legs weren't cut out, there was a white triangle of cardboard between them, and under her feet there was the crossed cardboard base that made her stand up. I cut the pink suit out, and put it on, carefully folding the white flaps around her flat shoulders, and then I decided to reenact the assassination. Paper dolls can't sit down, so although I managed to find an appropriate-sized car in my brother's room, Jackie sat in it, or on it, at a terrible angle, completely stiff and unnatural. I borrowed Ken from Barbie (Ken for Kennedy I thought, and the hair was almost exactly the same). He was slightly too big, and of course his plastic three dimensionality threatened Jackie's precarious hold on identity, but then he was the president. I took my arithmetic and geography books, which were thick, and put them in a pile, to make the Texas Schoolbook Depository, overlooking the motorcade, and I stole a little plastic soldier, lying down pointing a rifle, to be Lee Harvey Oswald. He was much smaller than Jackie or Ken, but that was O.K. because he was in the distance, a tiny little person shooting a gun. (Then I remembered Jack Ruby shooting him on TV, that was much closer, but Jackie wasn't there when that happened, this was Jackie's big day.) I found my green sweater and made a grassy knoll, and then I played Assassination. My sister sat on the bed and watched. Bang!! I took my crayons and colored in the red bloodstains on the pink Chanel suit, the one she wouldn't take off, the one she kept on, so that everyone could see the blood. Later I found some children paper dolls, to be Caroline and John-John, but they were almost as big as Jackie, so I gave up. The funeral was too difficult, I couldn't figure out how to dig a grave in the floor of my room, and anyway Jackie's wardrobe didn't have anything black.

He said: Widows do strange things sometimes. The woman who inherited the Winchester fortune, the fortune made from the Winchester 73 rifle, first her child died, and then her husband died, so she went to a medium, a clairvoyant, who said, you are being punished by the ghosts of all the thousands of people killed by the Winchester 73. The only way to protect yourself is to go as far away as possible, to California, and the only way to stop your house from being haunted is to make sure it is forever unfinished, forever being built, the sounds of the hammers must never stop. So she went out to San Jose, which was the middle of nowhere, and she built this huge useless house that was perpetually added to for thirty years, so that it makes no sense at all; she lived in it all alone, with builders endlessly working on it, money flowing, in continual payment, to keep it always unfinished. She didn't make plans, so the house is full of doors opening onto blank walls, or onto a drop of two stories, and staircases that go nowhere, and chimneys without fireplaces (she believed that ghosts come down the chimney like Santa Claus so she built lots of false and deceptive ones) and stained glass and skylights and amazing internal windows and holes in the floors and walls so she could watch her servants, she was sure they were stealing from her, because she was very very rich, and kept getting richer, because of course the rifle business went on doing well. And eventually, after her death, Walt Disney heard about this house, this spooky house with its crazed architecture completely obsessed with ghosts, and it became the prototype for the famous Haunted House at Disneyland. Of course Oswald used a Mannlicher Carcano.

She said: The Winchester 73 was the gun they used to wipe out the Indians; it would have been Indian ghosts whistling down the chimneys in San Jose. Up north in B.C., the Kwakiutl Indians think that every human being is the ghost of a salmon, or a whale, or a bear. It's not as if this simple animal stands in for a complicated person, but the other way around, the salmon is the most complicated thing of all, and when you die, the ghost jumps into the seas and the rivers, becoming a salmon again. It's like everybody is a ghost, and ghosts are jumping in and out of things all the time, changing their form depending on the situation and the time of year. And of course salmon really are complicated, even scientists don't understand how they work, because you know they have to find their way back to the very lake where they were conceived and born, spawned, out of all those fish eggs, they find that lake, and do sex, and die. It's amazing. As if we had to find the house, the bed, the back seat of the Chevy, where we were conceived, in order to fuck just once, and die.

He said: I saw a salmon ladder once, where they've built a dam, so the salmon can't get back up the river, and so they build a sort of wooden stairway up the side of it, with water rushing down, and the fish battle their way up the ladder, leaping against the rushing water, struggling to get to their lake, to die.

She said: It seems like sort of a wasted effort. The Kwakiutl Indians used to do potlatch; each band would spend all winter saving up and making carved boxes for the fish grease, which was their most precious thing, and lovely canoes and costumes and totem poles and collecting heaps of blankets, and then they'd have a potlatch which was like a big party, and all this wealth would be destroyed. Originally it was given away to all the guests, and then later, when they were all getting richer and richer (because the Anglos were buying furs and paying for them with Hudson's Bay Company blankets, red and blue, so that the blankets became like money, a kind of currency, so many hundred blankets equals one carved canoe), later in a final decadent version of potlatch they would just put all the things in a great heap and burn it. It was to show what a mighty chief you were, the more you could throw away, the more powerful you were. They thought of it as vomiting up the ghosts of all the things inside you, the stuff you'd eaten up, or consumed.

He said: Sometimes I think all the stocks and shares are the ghosts of the workers who lived and died working for those companies, and the Financial Times Index is like a salmon ladder, this completely artificial and perverse thing, and the shares go leaping up it, up and up, and then suddenly they come crashing down, to wreak terrible revenge on the rich people, like the Winchester 73 rifle ghosts.

She said: Yes, and the ghosts of all the workers shriek with pleasure as the market slides, and there's death and destruction and sacrifice on all sides, in this great global potlatch, and the ghost of the Azzedine Alaia dress jumps into the American Express card, and the ghost of the Porsche jumps into the filofax, and the ghost of the matte black bleeper jumps into the Cartier underwater watch, and everything is transmuted and transformed, and given away and destroyed and killed, in a great party at the lake at the end of the river!

He said: Can I have another mince pie?

She said: Gifts come back to haunt you.

He said: Giving something away is a kind of assassination. And when you eat something you've destroyed it, it disappears.

She said: The only way not to be haunted is to never finish.

He said: Whenever it's Christmas in the movies you always know something terrible is going to happen.

She said: Scary.

The wind howled in the dark night, singing through the leafless trees.

Toshiro Yamazaki

SONG OF MY SELF

This is a record of my experiments on my self.

——MONDAY——

I tried to drink LANGUAGE

I put LANGUAGE into a cup of tea and stirred well

I drank it and it tasted of forbidden fruit

One hour later, I threw up a great quanity of
Blood————————————Vivid Red

I was down in the VIVID RED SEA

————Rejection of LANGUAGE————

——TUESDAY——

I tried to eat LANGUAGE

I mixed LANGUAGE into a vegetable salad and put
VIVID RED SEA dressing on it

I ate it and it tasted of original sin

The next day, I had severely loose bowels

I saw the ALPHABET dancing on the bottom of the toilet

————Indigestion of LANGUAGE————

——WEDNESDAY——

I tried to wear LANGUAGE

I was in jeans and wore LANGUAGE next to the skin
instead of a shirt

It fit like skin and I felt identification
But I couldn't undress and I understood that it was
impossible to get out of LANGUAGE

Finally, I peeled off my skin with LANGUAGE

——Skin Meets LANGUAGE——

——THURSDAY——

I tried to sleep with LANGUAGE

I slept in pajamas and LANGUAGE was very quiet

I had horrible dreams all night long

The next morning, I found my self had been raped by LANGUAGE
and I noticed that my back had been carved with
the ALPHABET

——Offensive LANGUAGE——

——FRIDAY——

I tried to take a bath with LANGUAGE

I took a shower with LANGUAGE

LANGUAGE dissolved in water and streamed down the drain
I turned off the shower and laughed out Loud

I turned on the shower again, and LANGUAGE was
flowing with water

I poured LANGUAGE over my self and LANGUAGE never
streamed from my body

——Liquid LANGUAGE——

——SATURDAY——

I decided to burn LANGUAGE

I splashed Gasoline around my room and poured
Gasoline over my body with LANGUAGE

I set Fire to my self

I was surrounded by Fire

When I saw LANGUAGE was suffering Terribly, I felt a
GREAT JOY I had never felt before

I knew the End of All

——Agonized LANGUAGE——

——ONE DAY——

I revived

Now I was living in the Eternal Silent World

I revived as the Deaf, Dumb, and Blind

I was HAPPY

I got the Eternal Fact

No one disturbed My Self

    Even My Body

Will Staple

THE MORE I STARE

The more I stare
at waterfall
the more emotions fall
    off my face
the more
      "what's me"
is washed away
so the one behind
    my face is left
like the face of rock
the water
        falls
   over.

FERDINANDO CAMON

The Death of the Resistance Fighter

Translated from the Italian by Anthony Molino

There were times, in analysis, when a recurrent memory would surface without my knowing where or with what to connect it. It would come to mind often, and ended up prompting all kinds of associations. I'll try to tell you about it.

When I was small I'd occasionally see soldiers leaving for war. Two *carabinieri* would come looking for them, riding motorcycles, with draft card in hand and an injunction to leave. There were some soldiers, volunteers, who dressed differently from the rest. They wore black shirts. Before leaving, however, they would all go to church to be blessed. At the time I was unclear about the war, and against whom we were fighting. But one thing was clear: God was on our side.

A few years into the war, something happened in my hometown which greatly influenced my moral development. A resistance fighter, captured by the Fascists, was about to be shot. Flushed by dogs, he'd been hiding in a ditch when they caught a whiff of him and started racing his way, barking like mad. He jumped out of the ditch and climbed up a tree where, standing amid the branches, he raised his arms over his head. After taking him prisoner they led him to the piazza, where crouched against a wall for half a day, he was left in plain view for all to see. He wasn't from our town, and nobody knew him. I was six or seven years old then, and he was the first resistance fighter I'd ever seen. I expected him to be stronger; I thought resistance fighters were all great athletes since they always lived on the run. Instead, this one was very weak. He was leaning against the wall as if he didn't have the strength to get up. I remember thinking to myself: "Now watch him jump and run away." He never did.

There was a Fascist guarding him, walking around, with a cigarette in his mouth and a Beretta 38/42 in his hands. Every once in a while he'd stop alongside the prisoner, bend over, and blow smoke into his face. With the cigarette butt he'd burn his nose: the very nose at the source of my nosebleeds. I thought to myself: "Now he's sure to punch the German." Instead, it was strange, he batted his eyes as if they hurt, and stayed put. To throw a punch he would have needed his arms. But his arms were always dangling at his side, as if they weren't really arms but the shirt-sleeves of a mutilated man.

In the meantime, a jeep had made the rounds of nearby villages. A megaphone was used to announce that at 1700 hours, an enemy of the Italian people would be executed in the square. The jeep was full of men with black shirts, whom I believed to be blessed. They probably were. I also believed they had something in common with both my parents, that they were our boys, and that the bandit they'd captured was an enemy of ours. At 5 p.m. they start getting ready. They're all nervous, since not many people have come out to watch. They lift the prisoner up against the wall, only to have him collapse to the ground. So they leave him there. Then the priest arrives, approaches the prisoner, mumbles some words to which he gets no response. He gets up, and blesses the man with his cross. Which confused me. First he blesses the blackshirts, who are on our side, then blesses a resistance fighter, a man who is their enemy. The priest does everything calmly, with great precision. A Fascist runs up and tries pushing him away, and is joined by another one from the group. The priest continues to take his time: still holding the cross, he steps aside, a few meters to the man's right, stops, raises his arm and extends the cross towards the small group of Fascists about to shoot. It almost looks like they're shooting at him. The resistance fighter had been watching without a trace of emotion, as if he hadn't seen what was happening. But here my memory stops: it doesn't include the execution.

But these blanks, I've learned, often hide something real. The execution did take place, but changed nothing: the resistance fighter stayed right where he was, crouched on the ground with his arms dangling, his head hanging. You couldn't even tell whether they'd hit him or not; it was the same as shooting at a heap of rags. That image, of a man left to die like a pile of rubble, without a cry, without a twitch or a jolt, is the most frightening of the entire scene. Which is why I've erased it from my memory, without its leaving a single trace. But there's further proof to remind me that the scene did indeed take place, and that I was a witness to it.

Of the films on the Vietnam War, there is one in which a Vietcong is captured by a South Vietnamese patrol, brought to a village controlled by Americans, thrown to the ground against a wall, and shot. Watching the film, I said to myself as they opened fire: "I bet he won't even flinch." They shoot, and the man remains motionless. But he is dead. I know so, because I've seen it all before. They used a Garand, the most handsome and precise weapon in the world. The director of that scene had seen the killing of my resistance fighter.

History is a crime. Analysis is history on trial, with man as the main exhibit.

The Press,
Spurious Scholarship,
and Palestine

EDWARD W. SAID

CHRISTOPHER HITCHENS

ALEXANDER COCKBURN

These are excerpts from remarks made by Edward Said, Christopher Hitchens, and Alexander Cockburn at Black Oak Books, Berkeley, February 6, 1988. The occasion for the symposium was publication of *Blaming the Victims*, edited by Edward Said and Christopher Hitchens (Verso, 1988).

ALEXANDER COCKBURN:

When I first ventured some criticism of Israeli policy back in the middle 70s and found to my surprise my article immediately censored in the *Village Voice* and fairly soon thereafter became acquainted with the facts of life about writing about the Middle East, I was amazed initially at the solitude I felt as a press critic. And then gradually some important figures loomed into view, those who were providing the facts, the information, and the political sustenance that one needs if one is going to pursue this very heterodox line, certainly in mainstream American journalism. None more so than Edward Said. And also Christopher Hitchens. The fact that they have now jointly edited *Blaming the Victims* does, I think, now show that progress really has been made over this last decade and a half in ending what must be one of the more amazing periods of intellectual blindness, and moral blindness, in the life of any civilization that I can think of.

Cockburn went on to introduce Christopher Hitchens by quoting him:

"The conservative and neoconservative style as it is applied to American politics and the Cold War boils down to a simple injunction. . . . Whether the subject is nuclear war, terrorism, or Central America, and whether the dissent is of a pacifist, humanist, or socialist character, the dissenter swiftly learns that he or she will be met with the official injunction—"This is a democracy we've got here, so shut up!". . . .

What I have been saying about American attitudes can be applied with redoubled force to the case of Israel and the occupied territories. The United States pays, through a democratically elected Congress, the greater part of Israel's military budget. Its professors, journalists, and citizens circulate freely between the two capitals. It is linked to Israel by a thousand ties of affiliation. Israel thus presents almost the only instance where American activity by citizens, as well as by government, could have any immediate effect. *That* is why nothing must be done or said. Democratic practice is better when praised than when observed. As a result, Israeli politics has been slowly taken over by alliance of the militaristic and the messianic, and American intellectual and moral credit has been kept in the vault, the only safe place for it.

CHRISTOPHER HITCHENS:

I don't suppose anyone here will by now be unaware of Itzhak Rabin, or unaware of the order he recently gave to the occupying forces in the West Bank and Gaza to pulverize the bones, to break the limbs, and to mangle the hands of the insurgent Palestinian youths who have put an end, unaided, to the long period of suspended animation in which this topic has rested for too long. The bluntness with which Mr. Rabin expressed himself has been the occasion for considerable hand- wringing in what I think one can still call, without a deforming curl of the lip, "liberal circles." Does Israel not realize that it is supposed to be a light unto the nations? Does it not realize the high standards to which it must be held by American intellectuals? And so forth. And I think a partial answer to this question can be found in a chapter of our book. It's contributed by my friend Peretz Kidron, an expert Israeli journalist who also makes a living as a translator, and in that capacity translated Rabin's memoirs into English before they were submitted to the military censorship. In our pages are reprinted for the first time the chapters in which Rabin describes the expulsion by him at gunpoint of the inhabitants of the Arab towns of Ramallah and Lydda on the direct orders of Ben-Gurion in the year 1948. That's to say I think we can establish in this book something of a pedigree for the behavior of Mr. Rabin and remove at least *some* of the looks of polite incredulity that have formed at this apparently egregious statement on his part. Of course, other people have known Rabin in other capacities and not purely in his capacity as a persecutor of Palestinian nationalism. It was, after all, in his capacity as Israeli ambassador to the United States that in 1972 he so far departed from diplomatic propriety as to recommend that American Jews forsake their allegiance to the Democratic Party and give a second term to Richard Milhous Nixon, thus in my view earning another claim on our attention and putting a distinct stop to the idea that we are not free to comment on the affairs of the Jewish state or its internal affairs. The other reply to that, of course, is that the West Bank and Gaza are *not* part of Israel or an international responsibility. But as the taxpayers of the paymaster state for that occupation, we have an obligation to comment, and to engage ourselves, and to be free of the moral blackmail that is so often the answer to those who presume to criticize Israel and its doings.

Finally, of course, it won't have escaped your attention that Mr. Rabin and his colleague Mr. Peres were at the heart of all the dealings at home and overseas that we've come to know under the rather euphemistic rubric of the Iran/Contra affair. At every stage of the exchange of blood money for hostages, of further money for further murder and mutilation and devastation in Nicaragua—with one fascist regime washing the bloody hand of another— at every stage of the evolution of that nexus of violence and antidemocratic collusion were to be found Mr. Rabin and Mr. Peres, their organs of state, their antiterrorist expertise, and their police mentality. This, too, I think entitles us to move this issue somewhere quite near the top of the agenda.

Now, the internal affairs of Israel have also been pretty well internalized in American intellectual life. As a journalist, I'm quite accustomed to seeing bias displayed, usually, and I think not coincidentally, pro-establishment and conservative bias, in the discussion of any foreign policy topic that is placed before the public. But it's only I think in the case of the Middle East dispute that that bias can be represented as absolutely consistent and as having something of an organized character to it. I do not believe that on any other question a book like *From Time Immemorial* by Joan Peters could have been published. It is an *entire* concoction, a fabrication, a forgery, and a scholarly scandal designed to prove with phony statistics and bogus demographic evidence what cannot be proved in reality, that is to say, the nonexistence of the Palestinian people, people who weren't even around not to be expelled from their homes in 1948. I don't believe that such a book on any other topic could have received the accolade that it received from the *New York Times*, from the *Washington Post*, (from *cela va sans dire* the *Nouvelle Republique* or from *Commentary*) and from what we are pleased to call enlightened and educated opinion, a solid wedge of encomia. I don't believe that could have happened to any other book arguing any other case on any other subject. Just as I do not believe that in the case of an American military engagement overseas, a desperate struggle in a foreign country, a professor of linguistics at MIT could write the only extant book about it and have nobody review it at all, in a rather bold contrast to the treatment accorded to Joan Peters. I allude to *The Fateful Triangle*, Noam Chomsky's masterly description of the American intervention in the wake of the Israeli invasion and capture of Beirut. The only book on the subject—by an American, an American furthermore who can claim to be the only scholar of international standing produced in his generation—not reviewed at all. This is not just, shall we say, a want of impartiality; it's a thoroughgoing, consistent scholarly bias internalized by an entire community that fancies itself liberal, detached, and so forth. . . .

Now, by 1985–1986, the representations of the Arab in the American mass media had approached and surpassed the proportions of a bloody scandal. It was impossible to see the Arab represented as anything but *either* the bloated, hooknosed figure sitting upon a pile of ill-gotten wealth or the swarthy, unshaven, shifty, surreptitious terrorist and subversive. That these two caricatures are the *precise* imagery of European anti-Semitism I think ought not to escape those who *never* let pass an argument for the oppressed Palestinians, never let pass an argument for the rights of the Arab peoples, without making the attribution of that prejudice to us. And that the classic and base repertoire of traditional European Christian anti-Semitism should have been turned on the Arabs without a dissenting voice from the Antidefamation League, from the American Jewish Committee, about this maltreatment and slandering of their fellow Semites, seems to me to be also part of this.

This was the year in which, or the year after which, Walter Mondale, who carried the Democratic standard in the election, returned money from an Arab-American political action committee in Detroit on the grounds that his campaign did not accept Arab money. A sheer incitement to racism by the man carrying the Democratic standard. And even as we speak today and see the pulverization of Palestinian youth, the official published orders for brutality and torture, there isn't a squeak from Iowa, a squeak from the Democratic hypocrites who vie for the attention of you as voters and commentators. And I think it's therefore possible to say that anti-Arab racism is the only officially sanctioned racism in the United States, and while that remains the case, it is the racism we should worry about the most. Therefore, I want to say that our stand on this question comes without an apology.

Finally, and I say this with great modesty in the presence of Milton Wolffe, and I'm speaking now to the members of, shall we say, the socialist families so far as I can address them directly, those of you who consider yourselves on the left. The essence of being on the left, the thing that makes it important and worthwhile, the *sine qua non* of everything that is best in your politics, is internationalism. It's not just because of its moral superiority that internationalism is of the essence. It's not the attempt to prefigure a humanity that does not yet exist. It's not merely that. It's that if you betray internationalism, you will pay for it with your political life. . . . Internationalism is all we have got, and the consequences of betraying it are fatal. And the silence and collusion that is so regnant at the moment on the Middle East is, I think, a double betrayal of internationalism. It is of course a betrayal of the Palestinians, the oppressed people who have been silenced, deprived of the right to nominate their own negotiators, deprived even of the right to be considered as inhabitants and partners in the land of their birth. Obviously, a position that is congruent with that is a rejectionist position, and to hold it is to repudiate and defame any claim to internationalism. But it is another betrayal, too. It's a betrayal of the very courageous people in Israel—I'm thinking of people like Professor Israel Shahak and many others, some of them in the MAPAM Party, some of them independently affiliated—a betrayal of the many, many Jewish people who have taken it upon themselves to speak for the Palestinians, to defend their rights, to uphold their claims, to risk the opprobrium that comes with that, to risk the idiot cries of treachery and subversion that are visited on them. That must be hard, since they've suffered persecution in their time also, as Jewish people. The silence and collusion with official Israel betrays these people too. I think this double betrayal of internationalism can't be countenanced any longer, and I think that its vulgar reflection in the biased and distorted liberal scholarship that we've set out to criticize is no less of a disgrace.

East Jerusalem, 1988. Israeli soldiers and young Palestinians.   Photograph by Adam Kufeld

In introducing Edward Said, Cockburn quoted a letter from Said to the *New York Times:*

> The president of the Committee for Accuracy in Middle East Reporting in America, Winn Marshalman, suggests I am lying about the pacification of Gaza in 1971 and that, unknown to residents of Gaza or anyone else, conditions there have actually *improved* since the Israeli occupation. Moreover, she blames the Arab states, *not* the Israeli occupation, for the current insurrection. Let me quote from political perceptions of the Palestinians on the West Bank and the Gaza Strip by Ann Lesch, published by the Washington Middle East Institute in 1980. Her source for what follows is the *New York Times.* "On January 4, 1971, the Israeli military authorities clamped down on the strip. The Emir was summarily dismissed, followed by the entire Gaza municipality, which had existed under Egyptian rule, on February 15th. Twenty-four curfews were imposed on refugee camps, while Israeli troops made door-to-door searches, and the men from the camps were sometimes forced to stand waist deep in the sea while the soldiers pursued their hunt. Some 12,000 people were deported to detention camps in Sinai. In July 1971, the army began to thin out the refugee camps, demolishing almost forty houses daily in Jabalya, which housed 40,000 persons. Many of those who lost their homes were removed to el-Arish in Sinai. The army bulldozed wide streets through the Jabalya and Shati refugee camps in order to seal off and separate each section. After U.N. Secretary General U Thant protested against the demolitions and evacuations, the army temporarily ceased them. By then over 13,000 people had been uprooted." It would be difficult even for Jonathan Swift to have invented a precedent for accuracy in Middle East reporting in America who allows herself to believe that all the riots and brutalities of the Israeli occupation are the result of *better* living conditions for the Palestinians. Since not even the Israeli government has ventured such a preposterous argument, it leads one to suspect that both Ms. Marshalman and her organization are a bad joke. Surely the Israeli lobby can find better propaganda methods than this.

EDWARD SAID:

I want to speak very briefly about what has been obviously occupying the minds and bodies and hearts and eyes of many people, and no more so than those of the occupied territories, the Palestinians. It certainly is a momentous and extraordinary period. . . . It's interesting that some Israeli and, of course, Palestinian statistics show that there have been incidents on the West Bank and Gaza of somewhere between three and four thousand per annum in the past five years. So there's been a continual resistance to the occupation in all sorts of forms, most of them unreported by the media in the West, obviously because it was determined that the Palestinian issue was to be put on the back burner. With their usual acumen and powerful moral fiber, the Arabs concurred in this at the Amman summit in November, when it was revealed to the world that the primary agenda item for the Arab world was the struggle with Iran, waged by the gallant and enlightened kingdoms of Saudi Arabia,

Kuwait, the "democratic" Republic of Iraq, etc. With the concurrence obviously of the United States and other regional powers, including the Israelis.

I recall the day that the summit brought forth its wonderful communiqué. It suggested that the top issue was, of course, the battle against Iran, and against Shiism, and so on and so forth. This was greeted by the press in the West as an important change in the Arab world, that here, for once, for the first time since 1948, the number one priority in the Arab world had shifted from fighting Israel to fighting Iran. This was greeted on the Op Ed pages of the *New York Times* with a number of remarkable articles more or less echoing this line, saying that this was a historic turning point. A bare month later, less than a month later, the insurrection erupted in Gaza.

In trying to reconstruct some of the events, a number of things stand out—call them "vignettes," call them "apercus," call them "apocryphal stories"—that all reveal information suggesting powerfully convincing arguments for the strength and resilience of the Palestinian national movement, not only in the occupied territories, but elsewhere as well. You mustn't forget that since 1955, and especially between 1985 and 1988, there has been a bloody war against the camps, the refugee camps in Lebanon. The so-called camp war. . . . In any event, to return to the welter of incidents out of which one tries to construct a picture of what's happening, in Gaza principally but also in the West Bank, I recall one story I've heard from two people in the occupied territories, a man from Gaza and a friend from the West Bank, and then later from a Palestinian who lives in New York, the son of Palestinian refugees who grew up in a refugee camp outside Damascus. Recently I heard it again from a fourth person, and this is the story. A whole bunch of kids are throwing rocks at the Israeli soldiers. The soldiers pounce on one of these delinquent boys, an eight-year-old kid, and they grab him, and they have finally captured him. He runs away. They go after him, they hold on to him and they say, "Who has put you up to this? We're determined to find out." They shake him. He says, "Nobody, I did it on my own." Finally, after a good deal of shaking and cuffing and so on, he confesses. "It was Mohammed that put me up to this." "Where's Mohammed? Take us to him." "All right," he says. So, they march him off into the camp. Mohammed turns out to be his brother. They go to the house, they knock on the door. No answer. They smash the door down. The mother comes to the door and they say, "Is Mohammed here? He's your son, isn't he?" She says, "Yes." "Where is he?" "In the back room." They go into the back room and there's Mohammed. A six-year-old boy. Every time they find a leader there's a younger and more determined one behind him.

Here's another story. This was tremendously powerful and moving, because it happened to me. I was taking a taxi in New York about three

Gaza, 1988. Jabalya refugee camp.

Photograph by Adam Kufeld

weeks ago on a bitterly cold day. I was going only a short distance, in fact I had had a knee operation and couldn't walk. I got into the taxi and we went off towards 125th Street, which is where I was going, and the driver looked in the mirror and said, "Haven't I seen you on television?" I paused and said, "Well you might have." Then he said, "You're Palestinian, aren't you?" And I said, "Yeah." One always feels slightly, you know, worried about that. He said, "I'm Israeli." I thought, "Oh my god. Do I need this? on a cold day?" So I went on the attack. "Do you like it here?" He said, "Yeah, except for the crime." I agreed. "Yeah it's terrible, they broke a window of my car," which was true, "on Christmas Eve." He said, "It's terrible, you know, they've smashed my head; they tried to take my money."

I was, as you can see, trying to make small talk, I didn't want to get to the burning issue of the day. And then all of a sudden he said to me, "You know, I was a member of a unit that refused to disperse a demonstration on the West Bank, and I left." My heart melted. I just couldn't believe it, that this encounter with a Palestinian and an Israeli should be of this sort. So I said, "That's terrific." He told me, "You know, a lot of people think all Israelis are bad. We're not." I said, "I know that, I have a lot of Israeli friends." And so there was a brief warm handshake, and I got out of the car exhilarated that this man had seen what there was to be seen.

A third story is from a remarkable article about the insurrection by a Palestinian journalist who writes in Hebrew. (The people in Gaza say that the best people in Israel are the journalists who come into areas where they shouldn't be, and write the truth.) He writes a hair-raising account of a day in Gaza, the day he arrived, when the insurrection was in full swing. He soon discovers that there are leaders, regional sectional leaders, in the city, in the Strip, and they keep the pressure on all the time. He meets a man who is leading an insurrection—stone throwing, tire burning, screaming, and retrieving dead bodies from hospitals. (The Israelis try to bury the dead at night so the people can't come to the funeral where a new demonstration could develop.) And this man says, "We are *all* part of the national leadership of the 'uprising.'" People come from everywhere to give him information about an insurrection starting in such and such a place. He says they all go to sleep as soon as it gets dark and start their work at three in the morning. They go from three till sunset and, for the most part, the Israelis cannot control them. Now that is not the impression you get on television.

The curfews for example. On television and in the press, the cameras are always behind the Israeli troops, so the press shows the perspective of the troops, who claim they have accomplished these curfews, shutting down the camps all through the West Bank and Gaza. This man reports that it's simply not true. They shut down one street and something starts up on another, so the insurrection is going all the time. And the people in the camps create a situation the Israelis have not been able to control. They create what he calls "moving walls of people," two or three thousand people moving up and down the street throwing stones. And as you see these scenes, the main point that strikes every one of us, Palestinian or not Palestinian, Jewish or not Jewish, is that it is forbidden to be afraid. These kids—the Syrian poet Nizan Qabbani called them "the children of the stones"—go up front and start throwing stones. They're not afraid. They've grown up without any sense of the depredation and humiliation of earlier generations. And this constant pressure suggests that this is a national insurrection. I think it's momentous, it's dramatic, it's important, and the main message is that the Palestinians have *not* capitulated.

Everything has been against us in one way or another over the last twenty years. That is to say, there is a *wretched* Arab environment that cannot be trusted. There is a terrible international environment, in which our enemy, our principal oppressor, is guaranteed, lock, stock, and barrel, by a superpower. We have no such strategic or other kind of ally, and above all there is the geographical dispersion of Palestinian communities. Yet, somehow the communities stay together. They were brought closer together politically at the national council meeting in Algiers in April, which I attended, and all the factions are now proposing together a vision of the future based upon an exchange of land for peace. Arafat, despite the wretchedly unattractive appearance he presents on television, with his "mass-murderer dark glasses," his unshaven face, his impossible English, his writhing contortions, his massacre of English and every other language that I've—No, his Arabic is actually quite good — Arafat does say over and over again, "I challenge the Israelis to come to a peace conference." But this is not new. He has been saying it for years.

And where are the Israeli voices? They're there, but they're small and marginal. In the Israeli government, Peres is the great dove. Well, what does Peres propose? A peace conference, he says, but he won't talk to the PLO, he won't talk about withdrawal, he won't talk about recognition, he won't talk about sovereignty for the Palestinians. He won't talk about anything, really, except some condominium with Jordan. I mean, is this the great advanced Israeli position? Whereas, as all this is happening, the Palestinians are presenting proposals for peace, and the people all through the West Bank and Gaza, and Israel proper, have at last risen up. The lesson of it is that Arafat is a kind of symbol of the unity of the people. We all feel, whether we're here or on the West Bank or in Gaza or in Lebanon or elsewhere, that there is this national community, separated physically, but united in many, many ways.

The last point I want to make is that what we are watching on the West Bank and Gaza is obviously an intelligent movement now. This is a movement that is directed. Now, I think it would be foolish to say that it's directed from the outside. I mean, these idiotic speculations in the press: "This is incitement by the Muslim, by the mullahs, by the clergy. It's the mosque. It's the Muslim fundamentalists. It's rock-throwing individuals. It's nothing, it'll pass." This has been Rabin's message from the beginning, it's the work of "outside agitators," the common line we've heard in every conceivable mass insurrection. None of this is true. The fact is that there is an organization; there is an intelligence behind this uprising that has galvanized the entire community.

Where, by the way, are the people who have complained about Palestinian terrorism? Here is a people rising up en masse, straight out of the *Battle of Algiers*, and nary a peep, except here and there. We have to worry about the image of Israel, they say. It's not nice to watch Israeli soldiers beating up kids. It *isn't* nice. But the point is that our vision is *not* to throw anybody into the sea, not to kill, but to say we want rights for ourselves like you. We are a people. This is our land. And we want to be treated as a national community, not as some miscellaneous bunch of residents of the West Bank.

And what has the United States brought forth? In its inimitable way?

A proposal for reviving the peace initiative! Which is what? Not to deal with it. Not to deal with the representatives of the Palestinians. For years the United States has been looking for alternatives to the Palestinian representative, the PLO. All right, so others are found, but they're not acceptable because they are too extreme. So we deport them. Then we look for the moderates and moderates are not to be found; and when they *are* found, they're thrown out because they're too extreme. It's an endless cycle. So the United States has put forward a proposal, after all that's happened, for a limited-something-self-government, you know. And do they honestly think that these kids who are throwing rocks, the eight- year-old and the six-year-old Mohammeds, are going to be satisfied with a scheme that allows them *limited* self-government? Or representation by Hussein? And what in his wisdom is Secretary of State Schultz proposing? That Mr. Murphy should go and visit Syria and Saudi Arabia, the two most irrelevant countries in the world at this point. It is astonishing.

So, in sum, it is incumbent on all of us who live in this country, because this country is the principal party in terms of funding and support, to raise our voices. We should *make* it an issue, because the constant occupation by Israel is funded by the United States. The very day that Mr. Reagan said, "Naughty boys, you shouldn't do these things on the West Bank," he gave Israel another $200 million. The very day itself. So the struggle goes on. More of us must raise our voices and say: What Jews have got and should have—self-determination as a people in Israel—we should have. Because we were here first, and we are just as human as they are. And why should we, the victims of the victims, be denied what the victims have?

From a recording, courtesy of KPFA FM, Berkeley

REMINISCENCES

JONAS MEKAS

Translated from the Lithuanian
by Vyt Bakaitis and Roland Grybauskas

1

It was already summer, when we left Flensburg.
Sailboats filled the bay, and
out on the shoreline piers, over open water and the fishing boats
there was a shimmer of heat.
And once we'd made our way
out to Glücksburg,
the children there were noisily splashing
in a thick-grown forest of reeds.

We felt the pull of distance.
War was just over, with its last
shells, its last bomb blasts
still echoing off the slopes. Past stations in rubble,
and gutted, charred little towns,
we kept moving on, pushing our way in
among women and children,
war prisoners and miserable soldiers
squatted down in muggy heat, slumped together
with the swarms of refugees
on grimy floors, with hunger and thirst
to stretch our hands out toward any well
or cup of water,

In 1944, on the verge of being arrested for active resistance to the Nazi occupation, Jonas Mekas left his native Lithuania. Together with his younger brother Adolfas, he spent the intense final year of World War II, including a term at forced labor, inside a collapsing Germany. Having survived the war, the brothers stayed on in Germany, to join with several thousand displaced persons in making an unsettled, nomadic, ever transitional progress through various UN refugee encampments set up on the sites of former German military compounds, until eventually emigrating to New York City in 1949, before the dissolution of the camps.   [V.B.]

and snatch up tiny, under-ripe green apples
gritty and battered off railroad embankments,
or out of ditches below the tracks.

So, slowly, we pushed on that summer, laying in
at every trainstop, beside each bridge,
trudging down blackened knolls and
out along narrow field paths,
spending the nights on burned-out platforms
and charred tracks.

You remember. That time we were in Hanover,
sprawled out where the station had burned to the ground,
looking up at the bright night sky that June,
hearing those heavy worn-out ravings,
freight yard hoisting-cranes, the wrenching
sad city noises filled with uncertain steps,
with death and grief:

staring at a pale moonlit night
that felt so worn out, worked over, scorched
and shattered from what not long before had been the proud
core and center of Europe.

With eyelids dropping, the feeling gone
from each nerve end, we kept on pushing south that summer
through heavy rumblings, beyond exhaustion,
and each town, each horizon,
each train stop along the way
gave off a lingering stench of death and smoke,
now with broken-down, burned-out tanks and fortified trenches,
highways blown up
and bomb craters midfield — deep hollows
staring back black death —
the only scrawny vague
surviving witnesses
under the first flowers of spring.

On and on we kept pushing
through towns in rubble, past wrecked horizons
with villages razed, acres of cannon and truck,
whole graveyards of steel,
and squads of an occupying army,
their painted guardrails around town squares glaring white.

So we pushed on
and saw people starved down to nothing
come out from under the broken brickwork, in clusters
up from the dust, in vivid stripes of concentration camp inmates,
deathlike, their hands shrunk to nothing,
the women and children surfacing in swarms.

And the war prisoners. Ringed in by shabby, grimy barracks
they sang in a pale haze under the sun, played
cards while waiting for the last trucks, freedom
bound, to take them home.

There was one young German soldier, still a child,
all of a child standing there
inside the burned-out Hanau station, staring at
the heaped up brick and stone, the skeletal steel,
tree trunk, smokestack and dirt charred the same overall black,
windows wrenched out of their frames, a mesh
of iron and steel sagging down —
his childhood in shreds, all that was left of it.
Tears ran like water down his face,
just like water.

We had crossed salt marshes up north, desolate fields,
black Ruhr Valley skylines,
to push farther south, through dense
mid-German towns. So that

now it was August, maybe only
the end of July — time went and faded out —
we found ourselves in Würzburg.

It was still morning, yet the air
flared a real summer flame.
All tired out, we stood on a platform
and stared at the stubs of masonry left,
the rolling hills, the gold
summer shimmer:

and felt this sudden urge
to go out in the fields!
It was the pull of summer, the burning Bavarian sky
and sunlight —
and taking what was left of our memories with us,
our pitifew packings for the trip (the towel
mother made us take, a scarf from our sister,
some snapshots now faded), we were
suddenly high up inside the orchards.

Now here we were months later, after all that death,
eyeing orchard slopes, trees,
and villas that hugged the hillsides,
not believing any of it yet,
still full of the road we'd gone, the swarm
of pounding noises.
And yet these apples, ripe and full, were not the charred
green apples from the railroad tracks.
This was Bavaria we were in.

Look, my brother was saying: how green
the fields and trees all around!
As we climbed on up to the top of the orchards
and walked the fields
half crazed, drinking in the smell of wild roses,
the shade of the orchards.

This was life reviving, in every
apple bough and vineslope.
And the people, the
grown girls, women in gaudy summer kerchiefs,
with wicker baskets full, ripe as orchards
alongside the men, making their way down into town.

Dizzy with summer blossoming,
all that vitality, that vineland fragrance,
we sat there on a hillside, looking down
the deep track the stream of the Neckar had carved, and out
past the ruins of Würzburg, reflecting
on the years of suffering, death and despair,

and marveled at the life coming back — each sign we saw of it —
and the earth's strength.

2

Under a burning Australian sky
lies my Regina's grave. Burned by the sun,
with hot sands and cool nights like hands
caressing, keeping it safe.

Sleep, and go on sleeping, under your sky-blue eyes; not that
I'll get to see them again, any more than they'll ever see
our faraway childhood sky.
Still, I do keep them like two
tiny dew-beaded pearls.

That time we went together, one last time
across a flower-crested field, scanning
the hillsides for approaching rain,
then stopped in the doorway to a broken down old house
and watched a bright green, rain-
washed field,
shiny with beads of rain, and listened
to the thunder rumbling, the rain hissing in
over the hills.

Your eyes a rain-washed field,
two beads of rain.
Maybe I really
should not have taken your hand that time.
Maybe not, after all. Hands join like roots,
and not just to uncover lives.

Sleep, under the wide span of a silk horizon,
and go on listening to that strange balmy wind
gusting in through forests, level sands and lake tops,
all that way across briny high seas
and faraway islands —

still listening for that faraway echo of childhood,
the one voice your friends had in common —
while I keep on going, growing more and more remote.

And where, with your eyes open wide, so clear and childlike,
are you now, Marcele — left behind as you were
in some small nameless town in central Germany —
and you, Vladas?

The time I met you two, that spring,
sunk in the teeming green at Wilhelmshöhe,
guiding each other along past the falls
on your way down a gushing hillside in spring,
watching the high water, branches on trees,
you held hands all the while.

And it never crossed my mind, not once,
not even the time a whole bunch of us went singing
through flowering midsummer fields,
along the pale Wiesbaden streets —
I never once even happened to think . . .

the gray Hessen sky,
all the pale little towns, would stay so entranced, listening
for the approaching laughter, those sweet
friendships . . .

that it was all one woven into you all beauty
and love and suffering *sleep little one sleep*
while I keep going on to make my rounds complete

3

Again I see that powerful broad stream, one non-
stop shimmer of colors.

It was summer, that last time,
awash in sunlight, with bright rowboats
crawling slowly, singing and playing, past the islands,
bridges, castles hugging the slopes,
and everything shining back sunlit.

Now it's September, showing other colors.
The islands transparent, with leaves washed far out to sea,
cold foam breaks from the slow-plowing
dark tugboats,
their black shingled cabins spattered with rain,
smoke trailing into a cold, black streak
overhead.

With you the same old Rhine as ever, the wine
making men sing up and down both shores, still the same
long-haul sailors yelling down at grimy
toy boats, your birds
the same white hens perched on wooden
bridge posts.

No matter that the bridges gave out
under the crush of marching feet, or that the city chimneys
turned solitary rigid scarecrows,
you stay the same, as dark, as powerful,
carrying timber and white blood.

Without our gazing at the Rhine that summer,
or walking the bridge at Mainz, or letting ourselves go
in a fragrance of sunlight and roses down those vineslopes,
or making the Mainz-Kastel run on that tiny little train

with the basketloads of cherries and apples, white grapes
and yellow gold apricots;
somehow, without our being there, there'd be no trace of either
that summer or those days.

Still, it is strange how happy a summer that one was for us.
Even its bleak phases, for all our standing around with food parcels
or soup tins, had a shining
off the slopes and orchards and townships;
even while hanging out wash in the yards, or scanning
bulletins for the names of lost ones,
or grimly pacing the small squares
to track down each scrap of fresh news,
we kept a child's feeling for white Wiesbaden.

In going off to sit out a spell on some sun-drenched slope,
or down the banks to the Rhine to watch
the barges, down in that deep-carved track,
plod by under full loads of coal and timber
along the floodlit banks,
vinyards, bridges in rubble under water,
with the last war blasts
echoing off the slopes.

Even while sitting in some low, cool, beer hall off the marketplace,
scanning notices posted on walls, taking the cool summer air
with a pale green Rhine wine — hearing the farm horses
and girls in clogs clop by over the cobbles

down narrow alleyways — all the while drinking in
a chestnut-and-apple smell.

4

Early that fall, mid-September already,
with the rains just starting, we left Wiesbaden.

Mud was waiting for us, when we got to Kassel,
along with the white-washed wooden barracks, that autumn.
Trudging cold water, while the wind and rain
blew right through us,
we patched cracks in the barrack walls,
gathered up rain-soaked alder sticks,
and talked cold weather, mud,
oncoming winter.

And it was not much later
the snow arrived,
fuming in over the Wilhelmshöhe ridges and tree lines.

Yet winter, even that one, passed;
soon it was summer, then one more fall
coming on, as we watched the woods go under, out on the slopes,
while we stood by the trolleys,
or with our skimpy pouches
waited in long lines for bread,
milk and vegetables,
or tugged at carts coal and alder logs
loaded down.

Past thrashing and screeching from a pond inside our compound,
where children splashed unsettled black water on each other,
we'd stroll the schoolhouse footpath
hand in hand, in pairs or clusters,
and passing the commissary along the way we'd hear
strokes from constant, ongoing Ping-Pong inside,
the voices of Sipas and Tony, old records, an accordion wheezing.

Sundays, we'd go roam the fields,
or just stand around, down by the playing field,
to watch the men tossing a basketball
get worked up over each point,
or sit back inside our low-slung shed of a movie house
to watch some cheap slapstick, and then
pour out shouting, the whole slew of us
flooding one hillside,

while down below in the Yugoslav hall
harmonicas played and the dancing went on, while
frog-croaks carried across the fields and down through
gardens where people wandered the hedgerows and bushes
as solitary dreamers
to look off toward a blazing shimmer of lights
in faraway Kassel and listen
to the trains go pounding by,

until one day, toward spring, the departures started.
Saying our goodbyes, kissing each other
as old friends down the years having shared the long haul,
one room, one fate,
we carried out our pitifew belongings,
out bits and relics,

and climbed up into the trucks to look back
from under the canvas top at friends who were to stay behind,
eyeing their small cluster,
the few faces there, people standing
lined up by the edge of the lot, already starting to fade back:

and listened for the last time
to the noises of the compound, and looked at the barracks,
that cloud of dust off the road a last cover
hanging back there, obscuring the years,
the friends and the past, our shared memories:
looked out from under the canvas,
eyes steady, fixed on the road.

5

Schwäbisch Gmünd, and Wiesbaden;
Flensburg, Husum, the Heidelberg heights,
bridges, trees, rivers,
hillsides and market wells,
places and people —

there is this urge to see all that again:
the men playing, hollering inside the compound,
Tony bent over his bucket of whitewash;
to hear all those cherished familiar voices,
Sipas and Kestas, Yuya yelling,
the people sprawled out in shade
over by the apple trees in a small meadow;

and yet, Mrs. Marija,
it's you I think of;
you as well, Aldona and Birute;
Rasa; or Otis, hurrying off to the village
with a jug of milk, playing with your daughter under an apple tree:
I think about all of you, now.

Somehow there seemed to be more sun that summer
with us out there, walking
the slopes and margins of the apple orchards,
or settling down beside a stream,
so free and easy, right in the heat of the sun,
to lay out the shuffle for some game or other, —

it's later on we climb the hill and go
deeper into the forest, one sparse canebrake to the next,
yelping, screeching over each single raspberry we find,
then take our snapshots / each one at least had to have trees
and a rye field in it / —

and get back late that evening, tired out, sunburned,
to see the men still out there in the lot,
still wearing their green trunks,
yelling and hollering, tossing the ball around,

and carry back our choice handfuls of raspberry blossoms,
wild flowers and leaves.

6

Somehow or other everything scattered, thinned out all the faces,
summers, hands.

That fall we walked the fields, watched
the last autumn gold,
picked the last flowers,
and with the din of the camp left behind us
could see the wash strung up white in the compound fade
back there by the dormitory walls.

The fields were cropped already. Our talk was of home,
of rowanberries and cobwebs. And how really clear
that blue sky was.

We walked the slope down to a creek,
then waded the creekbed midstream,
while Jonas — funny, somehow — kept insisting
he was all set to haul us up a crab.

But we went on. And the farmboy he was
broke himself a branch and slashed the air as he kept up with us,
humming some tune only he could make out.

Stretched out for the spell of real heat, listening in on
the last fall days still close and hot
with insects and flies buzzing,
we just lay there in the shade. And with our heads turned up,
how blue everything looked.

We'd look down on the camp spread below us,
the town and the woods, the last gold cover,
and soak up that last summer quiver.

For once, just one time more, to be together
and hear familiar voices laughing, to go
roaming the fields free and easy again!

But then, in time, comes one last time for holding
hands, and a time for the leaves to start coming down.

Paulius, oh Paulius
where are the birches now, those white midnight birches
we danced around, down by the snackbar that time we were drunk on
    night,
with all of us hand in hand,
those white midnight birches,
those compounds all long since cleared out.

7

Here I am again, sitting in shoreline sands,
sifting memories like yellow sand,
soaking up summers past,
sun, sand and friendship
over and over.

And I can feel each hour,
each thing I touched, each
person, horizon and tree
become rarer, not ever to be torn out again,
with roots to clutch each memory
right at the core.

Who knew why, while we sat there that summer
under the spruce trees (with more guests than ever to attend to
and the radios on inside, with all that talk to listen to,
we sat out under that spruce
playing some game I no longer remember,
while our talk touched on one thing then another)
somehow it all seemed so routine then,
plain everyday: the music, the sun
and the game we played; not at all the way it looks now,
that far back: one big Sunday
drenched in sun.

And so the three of us would be standing
in pale sand, down on the beach,
tossing pebbles, or just sitting there
as evening came down and the summer place turned gray,
listening to it rain,
the branches roaring, the spruce trees soughing outside.

There was Sunday calm the next morning.
And we made it down from the lodge
to the bay sunk in early morning fog, where
motorboats hooted and wheezed,
and it was there we stopped to look out at the gray
tiny beachfront cottages
scattered along the morningside bay.

There was a day the horseback riders came.
From early morning on
you could hear their horses snorting, the riders
buzzing with talk over breakfast, boisterous,
free and easy; snapping their
red riding crops, later on,
as they walked the path through the woods.

While we sat on the big porch,
lounging back in our chairs, feet out,
to follow the new guests in, or said our goodbyes
while seeing each of them out the door,

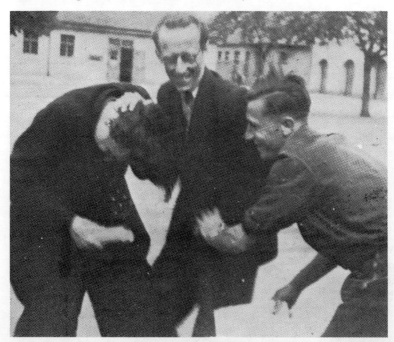

watching each car
pass the bend in the trees and vanish,
then turn back to our long hours, sitting
out on the porch (with all that sun there)
to gossip about the guests, or read
Dylan Thomas, or leaf through back issues of Collier's
(Master Bernardas sat outdoors
on the plank bench under a tree,
looking off somewhere past the branches
while he heard the trees roar)
meanwhile, we'd say: look at the cronies
those green lawnchairs turned into,
stuck in a circle under the trees.

There was the day Pranas stayed over.
He was like a maniac, hopped up, laughing;
with everybody somehow manic,
what from, whether sun, young blood, woods,
was hard to guess.
With Vida and Nijole hand in hand,
and Giedre along, talking something over,
picking leaves off the branches, all of us went on
down the path together, deeper and deeper into the woods.

There was little time that summer,
with the guests always there, either coming or going,
and yet that one Sunday we took off,
ran out on all the diners and made for the woods,
the four of us wading the sand,
and went on through the brush, singing, carefree,
sitting out on the beach among the dunes that evening,
looking off at the night sky.

Then there was the rain. Chopping into leaves,
drumming the rooftop, spreading huge streams
over the whole
summerhouse. We'd spend hours sitting inside,
with the few guests left, old friends by now,
Mrs. Valeria and her little boy, Rimvydas too, the time
we put in sitting inside that gray summer place
to hear rain gusting the branches
of spruce trees out in the yard,
keeping the talk low among ourselves,
thinking back some, then easing off,
letting the night take over
in one drowning surge, and so letting go.

8

You remember, Mrs. Marija, that summer we
took our long walk out by darkening summer streets,
down one hillside, our talk touching now this
now that — with Alda and Birute along,
gathering wildflowers and forest leaves by the fistful
into their arms;

and you, Paulius — all of you carefree,
untouched by pain, children still; you
birch trees in the middle of the yard, pale witnesses
to nights gone by:

remember how long a time
we stayed up that night, out walking, drinking cokes
at the snack bar, then all danced around the birch tree together?

You too, my white Meyence,
the heavy freight and merchant ships,
the smoke and wet spray,
Bremerhaven.

Where is my home, my country, my native land?

Horizons and towns, bridges on rivers,

salt marshes up north, windmills,
and wide-ranging autumn fields.

Each smell I came across I carried out with me,
each thing and sound, each frail
fragrant touch the fields and rivers gave off,

taking everything along, right from childhood on,
restless, with the same hunger gnawing, still
eager for each new meeting,
each streetlight.

Oh the head-spinning vastness you are, America,
with your red mountains, lush streams,
your garish cities laid out
in endless rich valleys
by riverside or oceanfront,
your rumbling harbors and fiery
ear-splitting steeltowns!

You, New York, with your ringing glass hands
immersed in soft cloud banks one
endless rain, with your harsh
interminable streets, your longing
wound around every one of my hours,
for each street and dockside,
all the squares and parks!

Bear Mountain, Hicksville, Lake Iroquois,
the tiny little cottages at Stony Brook
/ remember that time one morning we looked
down from the lodge we could feel
every minute already lived
sink deeper in, no longer to be torn out
for being lived through, yet now fully felt, like
something your own you cherish the most,
like home /

Home. Home. Each place,
each horizon, meeting and face:
each stop to look
a tie to home.

Didn't we sing our longing then,
drifting out on Lake Iroquois — even as your
flax-blue eyes, Leonora, moistened and filled
with a young girl's dreams?

As we listened for the calm across the lake, and stared off
at a shoreline of trees, and splashed the surface,
the past forgotten, along with time,
that living moment —
or while sitting near Camp Oscawana and gazing
at the Hudson, the blue rolling hills,
the Connecticut night filled out and spanning a century
of silence — weren't we then under
the spell of night and nothing else?

And later, having made our way down to shore,
we sat together on the beach and sang
softly, just for ourselves,
now we so inseparably merged with
the night and the shore.

Tell me, Leonora, were you thinking of home that time?
Looking off at pale level coastlines
and green horizons, that evening — / The upper deck
full of people, some dancing, someone singing
and playing banjo, we stood by the railing
and listened to the music, looking out at the flaming
bend of the Palisades to take in this dizzying, mystic
and painful American night,
so lulling and hypnotic in its relentless grip,
one drowning pull to wear memories down,
tear away at longings, times past, as it goes dragging
clear up into itself, to its core /
while someone kept on playing banjo
there was singing and dancing, with the fiery
bend of the Palisades burning, and the nightlights on in New York / —

Now wasn't each place,
each stop a look, and each and every instant
home?
Wasn't it painful, each time we split up,
and wasn't that home?

Or was it all just binding ties,
just binding ties and separations?

Don't ask. It's not as if I had any way of telling.
Hungry and thirsty still, with eyes just as eager,
unquenchable, drinking each new horizon in,
each face and river, all the squares and bridges,
with the same ties to everything, still the same
pain and torment in letting go:

so go on falling down, white
snow of times gone by, while I keep going
on and on, wherever my travels take me, to whatever strange
new horizons, cities and people —
the same pangs reviving, each time I let go.

Now go on falling down, white
snow of times gone by, while I keep on
going wherever my journeys lead
moving on and on, each time
without knowing what for, or where to —
not knowing, and not knowing — just the heart
pushing on, eyes squinting into the distance
for each blue smoke trail, each
new tree and face:

but no

it's not that tree, not the blue of that sky,
no not the face,
no not the smoke.

Sorrow, sorrow, sorrow.

Richard Silberg

TIME FOR OSIP

Stretched out here
leaping on the red divan
against the background tone of History
wires humming
                across the painted land
Everything is moving faster and faster
except for our flesh
which lives and dies along
at the old mammalian pace
Remembering you,
                Osip Mandelstam,
the words singing nervously
racing in your skull
the Word
leaping like Gothic arches
green and yellow
twining upwards into your stone
                        life

Are you dancing
                now,
little saint,
in the sun's arrow rays?

and what of wrinkled raisiny us, mon cher,
living in the flatlands, dying back
                resorbed like veggies
in our bank loans and children
us, bleating here
dwarfed against the gleaming lines and smokestacks?
This transcendance is a trick
                yes, Osip?
Forms wrestling against forms
the grand Design
we are as separate from it
as the individual cells of our bodies
are from the Brain

Whales are washing up on the beaches,
              more and more each day,
    Aurelio Rodriguez
had his head squashed off, yesterday,
      by a garbage truck
and as he was cooling into immortality
someone dashed across the street
    like a ballboy at a tennis match
to pick his pocket

But then, Osip, you never had an easy time
NKVD agents lurking in your bookcases
Stalin and his cowcatcher moustache
            always grinning in your borscht
Just, perhaps,
that things weren't moving quite so fast
There was Progress, yes,
the great hamburger machine
          of the First World War
mechanical cadres were emerging
planned societies
the landscape changing and thrumming

But now, Osip,
Christ,
things are electronic
They're not frozen, anymore, in sequential moments
the lines are fluid
stretching like a single Cell
shining oily black in unimagined shapes
like the poison sludge
creeping in, inexorably, year after year,
towards Long Island

We are so aware of these rising forms
the whales dying in sad pods
          underneath the sea
it's as if we could leap out of our flesh
rolling pinkly on the Wheel
just leap out and take an escalator ride
join you, Osip,
        in History

Only you're probably not even there, are you?
You're probably just dead

All that's left of you are words
words rasped clean of flesh
Your poems are like shells
fleshless
so pure in their death
      we can almost hear them sighing
and Time
Time pumping through them

Volker Braun

WALTER BENJAMIN

IN THE PYRENEES

Translated from the German by Anselm Hollo

To stride calmly into the wall of fog.
His arms swing, not smoothly but regularly.
Exactly pursuing the paper above the abyss.
In his briefcase explosives, i.e.,
The Present, *Die Gegenwart*

Step by step, as chance
provides narrow foothold
in the material. My dear lady, *not* to go
would really be taking a risk.
Keeping track of time / after five lines, a rest.

Fields in which only madness proliferates.
To push forward with the axe in your head
I have nothing to say. Only to show.
In the smallest, clearly defined segment.
Without looking right or left, onward
into the horror

By this method, I'll manage.
The vineyard's slope crumbles, slides
becomes horizontal, full of almost ripe
dark grapes. The briefcase the most important
thing! Body among the vines, panting, heart

struggling, the critical moment:
when the status quo threatens to last.
Dead bones below, vultures above.
Shorter steps, longer breaks.

My patience renders me invincible.
To set the sails of concepts. My dear,
may I help myself? At the summit,
suddenly just as expected the force

of the view. Deep blue seas:
suddenly, I see two. Cinnabar coasts.
Below the cliffs, freedom.

. . .

Entry denied at Port Bou. But we, the homeless
carry—would you mind holding the case—
the deadly dose with us.

He probably thought he wouldn't be able to manage that ascent one more
time. In the morning, the border officials found the corpse in my text.
Construction assumes destruction. The heavy leather briefcase, saved
from the hands of the Gestapo, *unos papeles mas de contenido
desconocido*, was lost. Too hasty, sir, that final stroke of the pen. The life
carries the work, if I may say so, up this almost vertical slope.
In every work, there is that spot where we feel a gust of cold,
like the dawn, coming

(Material XIII)

James Brook

PARIS SWEET

Il faut être plus cool dans la vie

Regard the visage in the glass—
it's hers, as expected. My friend
with money to burn, timed to kill.
Romantic, we were reading jokes
off my lips and the word *scud*
made a place for itself, let's say
a refuge, in the conversation.
Yes, the roads leaving the major
foreign city were Englished.
Snapshots of typical markets and
popular bistros. And the Canal
St. Martin was one thing. We kept
saying hello and examining the
signs for a sign; then, almost
at the last moment on the last day
of the long summer weekend, she
turned and said, "Hold me."

La Fête nationale / Bastille Day

First a personal note: God gave everyone in the better neighborhoods
teeth, it's said. But that night we felt just too immortal and didn't even
floss; *and* we neglected our prayers to the poet Jacques Prévert, the
coauthor of us all. Feigning insouciance and saying suddenly funny
things, we lingered at your showerside, smooching. Rivulets ran through
tresses, fingers dipped in transient pools, appreciation of birthday suits
continued till I made you—no, persuaded you—bedward past
windowsful of habitual spies. *Sound does not exist in a vacuum*, and the
air was ruled by prime time . . . sleek fighter planes extracted loyalty
oaths from summer thunder. That's not what made us happy, nervous,
adulterous, delighted.

Bousculade / Push Comes To Shove

A reasonable investment impartial
Impatient of automatism

A lead body rocks way back
A squeaky wheel begins to stink

Exactly not okay and awake
Serious elbows keep track

Toi qui étais au travail / While You Were Out

Elements of confusion were that day the same as us fat really fat and dancing as reported.

Minimum arcades.

So clouds shifted shuffled sniff-sniff—hardly!

Whenever I as far as Belleville.

Grab anything perfectly suggestively photographed, singly or in twos and threes.

Mayakovsky Writes From Moscow

Our unrandom collision mightily squeaked out
The fictional song of impending joy
Great broadcast choruses went into rehearsal
Advance tickets were snatched up by scalpers
Tuxedos were not to be had at any price
And ladies young and old fiercely
Competed for hairdressers' attentions
In frenetic prelude to our celebration

Then catastrophe struck
In fact your début's been canceled
Due to
Due to what
It really doesn't matter
A little calm please
No need to get excited
If even now the posters are coming down
Because
Because who knows why
I lingered eight days by the dumbfounded phone
Counting the minutes till your next call long overdue
A call that never came
O Maria I'm afraid my hands tremble
My jokes aren't funny my friends are annoyed
And shake their heads counseling
A closer look at local talent

"Work is the answer," swore Baudelaire
Okay I'll try
Anything to get my mind off it
Anything to get some relief
So secreted in the darkroom
I carefully enlarged your photographs
There had to be a chemical clue
In dust-oppressed libraries
I undertook serious research into various 'ologies
And after several eternities of scholastic cogitation
I nearly succeeded in reinventing reasons
For all your actions both manifest and latent
A jealous philandering husband got my first consideration
But other possibilities a glowering boss
A wildcat strike at the P.T.T. or the hazards of Paris traffic
Came to mind and kept me therapeutically busy

Still this much is unavoidable
The phone really has stopped ringing
Though today I think I got the message
Which I note here *There is no message*
Allez allez tu m'as dit la dernière fois
Dejected I turn to the round of days
Ticked off at dull work and to nights far worse
And to dreams encumbered by the chiming in of
[balance of manuscript unclear]

Envoi

Since "traveling doesn't interest"
Her.

Go. Just
Go.

MY ENEMY

MELODY SUMNER

When my enemy calls, I ride a fat ape to the red cell chill hour and reject her hypothetical isms for sanities coeur. She rides her mania's mechanism to the farthest gate. She messages minutes too late. She is far too out to lament or erase. Obsession is her weapon. She is memory's open flame.

(1) I spent the morning at my enemy's house. She had called earlier asking me to go there, get the key from under the railing at the top of the back stairs, use the key to open the front door, climb the stairs and enter the kitchen to find the pan she left heating needlessly on the open flame.

(2) I spent the morning at my enemy's house. She wasn't there. She was at the place where we both work on certain days. I got her the job when we first met and I didn't know yet what form our relationship would take. I trained her to work in my place. My work now depends on the efficiency and accuracy of what she does. Whenever she makes a mistake, which is often, it reflects on me, I am blamed.

(3) I spent the morning in my enemy's house. I noticed things. The furniture is sparse and eloquent in a classically spiritual style. Drawings made by her children are scotchtaped to the wall. Earlier this morning I was home, working alone, undisturbed until seized by the interruption of my enemy's call. Will I go then and prevent her house from catching fire? It's impossible, I protest, I am extremely busy right now. But who can resist the request of an enemy brought, if only for an instant, to her knees. She called me this morning because she couldn't think of anyone else.

(4) In my enemy's house I open every door and drawer, gorging on the variety of intimate detail in a house unprepared for the eye of the enemy. Throughout the rooms, Tchaikovsky's Sixth sounds. Here, the kingdom of the father is space. A blue vase contains seed. A windowless window frame hangs on the wall. In the closet, two mute shoes confide a striking devotion to their wearer's feet. Outside on the highway cars grind and growl.

(5) I spent the morning in my enemy's house. I am in love with her children, especially her daughter Magellan. Magellan is nine years old and has had her holes all sewed up so she will remain a virgin forever. At least that's what she tells me. Magellan is an emperor. Magellan is a conqueror. She's a fisher of men and women. Her mother disagrees.

(6) I spent one evening with my enemy's daughter in a boat during a

storm off an islct in the northern sea at the first light of the midnight sun. Someday I'll tell my enemy about that night . . . how Magellan's clear small voice kept me rowing as she read to me from a book about strip mining while waves piled high one on top of the other and the boat tipped riotously and the wind stinging ice and I'm rowing and rowing but we seem to be going backwards, farther out to sea.

(7) My enemy makes love with the devil. But first she pictures his eyes being gouged out with sticks. My enemy converses with angels. Speaking in twenty languages, she rents a boat named "Die Move" and sails alone to the ends of the earth looking for the window. Her heart is helmeted. Blue light streams in her bedroom at night.

(8) To the ancient Egyptian, the brain had no special significance. It's the heart that houses the soul. My enemy understands this. She removes the brain of her husband through his nasal passages. Then she removes his entrails through an incision she has made along the fold of his groin. She replaces these things each morning before he awakes, and removes them again each night. Her husband knows nothing of these practices, and wouldn't believe it if he were told.

(9) This is how my enemy appears in my dreams: She stands with her eyes directed forward, unfocused, her arms straight at her sides. She has a plain, impressionless beauty—smooth skinned, moon-like. Her face rides on the restive bulk of her frame like an iron buoy on a stone-still sea. Her flat brown eyes press into me, making me want to look away. When I summon my strength to meet them, her eyes shift back and forth with metronomic regularity. Her eyes have the power over mine to make them linger, but my eyes, my intention, is to make it impossible for her to look back once I have met her gaze.

(10) In one dream I am in a basement room with some friends, in the house of our employer. My enemy enters. She has arranged to meet with our employer to discuss renting the room for herself and her daughter. She and her husband are to separate, and their son will live with him. The ceiling is low, there are a few pieces of worn furniture, two good windows look out over the back yard that drops away to an exquisite view. The room has one door that is an entrance or an exit outside. My enemy stands in the doorway surveying the room. I notice dark stains around the inside edges of her mouth. Her eyes are dull, she's wearing a see-through blouse. She tells us she's been hanging out in bars all afternoon. This makes me sad. She isn't quite ready to make the move, she says. I feel sorry for her. She has been alone for centuries it seems to me. As she leaves I get the impression that she doesn't care what anyone thinks.

(11) In one dream, I tell her what I think of her. I tell her that I am not impressed by her belief that everything she does is ordained by a higher order. I tell her I have at times forgotten myself, I have done things equally dumb, but her actions seem to me to be cruel, self-destructive, and inconscient as well. As for her

assertion that she no longer has any interest in romantic love, I say it's quite the opposite—her fixation on my husband with the attending disregard for my feelings and those of her husband indicate that she has fallen victim to an infatuation of the most adolescent type. During this speech I observe her reactions with equanimity. She sobs ostentatiously. I tell her again that I feel she has been arrogant, selfish, ungrateful, and I explain why. She abruptly stops crying and starts to laugh.

(12) In another dream I am discussing important business matters with a very rich woman who is wearing a fashionable gunnysack dress and jewelry made from candy and donuts slung rakishly across her shoulders and choking her wrists. A beautiful woman, tall and dark, comes through the room asking for my enemy, "the deep one" she calls her. This makes me mad.

(13) In another dream my husband and I had been spying on two people involved in a very carnal act just before we were to deliver something like dryer lint to my enemy at her new place of work—a huge warehouse structure—where the substance would be made into pink, grey, and white paper in a process only my enemy understands. My husband carries the stuff in a film negative box. I lie down in the dirt quite a distance away and watch him walk up to her. She tries to prolong the contact but he turns and starts back.

(14) In my enemy's house Blaise Cendrars writes "To the End of the World." He eats raw peas and watermelon and watches soap operas with my enemy in the afternoons. She is interested only in keeping the flame alive. She goes into the closet with a blue window and counts to seven hundred using some other part of her mind. Objects are not treasured, they are revered, and bestowed with such authority and wisdom as are rarely attributed to their living counterparts. All day and all night people come by to look at the house. The price has not been set. My enemy and her family are squatters. They gained entrance to the house through a phone call made by a friend of a friend back east. No one knows where the real owner has gone. They may be forced out at any moment or they may be able to live there a thousand years. They like it that way. The uncertainty sets their votive resolve. When someone rings the bell, there is no sound, they've disconnected the circuit.

(15) Now, I must be fair and give a more complete picture of my enemy. Like many people, her heritage threatens to become her fate. This is the great engagement of her life. She was born to a passionate, impoverished woman, and a cruel, proud, and selfish man. They separated early and often. At sixteen, my enemy made her escape and met others like herself. More and more she retreated inside a rapidly diminishing space. At twenty, she gave birth to a devoted daughter to keep herself in this world. Pride of character inherited from her father was the enduring placemat upon which she set her plate. Self-indulgence inherited from her mother marked her voluptuous body and her sen-

tient face. She told me once she had always been *too* attractive. It caused a lot of trouble. Boys in high school would line up to watch her pass. She didn't feel right in that body, being stared at and lusted after all the time. But she knew she could have any boy she wanted. And that kind of knowledge once gained by the body is hard to erase. Even now at thirty—heavy, lassitudinous—her body retains a clear understanding of its power and speaks direct to man's appetite. Her husband's attempts to keep her dowdy backfire. She seeks the revival of her beauty's reign in other ways.

(16) It is not necessary that I forgive her trespasses simply because she has been trespassed against. Though I am capable of it, I did her no injury. I am innocent of all but flattery, vanity and pride.

(17) In my enemy's early border days she rode a tawny mare named "Caballo de Przewalski" with the advance guard past the outpost of Khorgos. She was just nineteen, and one of the finest soldiers in the far left frontier state. Her three year post in a small village on the hot, dusty plain of southeast Khazakhstan came to an end when she was implicated in an unusual scandal. She was abruptly transferred to remotest Cerski on the far north coast.

(18) My enemy has survived hardship, invasion, tyranny, revolution, repression, isolation, and life without the vote. Her landscape is immense, starkly forbidding in its luxury. She desperately desires autonomy but is forced to rely on others for her basic measure. Her

strategy is paranoia based on memory of fact. Secretiveness, self-righteousness, alienation, and self-deception are her preservation. Though she likens herself to the opposite, she embodies failure and loss. Her overriding concern with internal problems ensures that they persist. Her hexagram is strength divided by weakness, like a large tree branch that cannot support its own weight. She is firm, fixed, and courageous. Merciful, not empathic, she is closed, mistrusting, spurious, and resolute. Unbending, she invites collapse, and yet she stands.

(19) As for me, how often have I received approval for my most niggling deeds. I was never beautiful, but industrious, intelligent, openminded, and forthright. I was adored by my forefathers, to them I represented hope. The "cherrybowl bringer" I was sometimes called. My hexagram is weakness surrounded by strength. My weakness is made of these qualities: naïveté, forgetfulness, idealism untested, excessive sympathy, desire to be liked, ignorance of internal problems, blind fear, indulgence in anger resulting from wounded vanity masquerading as unselfish concern. I'm like a river with fortifications on either side.

(20) However, the "unusual scandal" was never referred to in any official documentation about that period. Her record was blanched and her name made good as abruptly as the charges had been brought on. Tales of her feats on horseback, her prowess at fighting, her steadfast bravery, and courageous deeds are recounted by many. Any at-

tempt to affect a recrudescence of the controversy surrounding the scandal has been met with sanctimonious disapprobation. Those who have persisted with investigations have been silenced.

(21) My enemy's name means "winner."

(22) My name before I was married translated directly as "one who prepares food." I changed my name with marriage and now my function is as a messenger, that of summoning others to a higher self. My enemy didn't change her name with any of her marriages. Her family coat of arms is based on knighthood, magic, and the number three.

(23) The story continues like this. She gave birth to the daughter several high priests had predicted would become an important figure in the heralding in of a new age. Strangely, from the beginning, the daughter exhibited all the qualities her mother seemed intent on banishing from her life.

(24) Jesus is rumored to have said, "It is more blessed to give than to receive." It is also more difficult. A gift is no gift if it bears a hidden price. I was incontinent with my charity. It soiled my intercourse even with strangers. My enemy saw this. She discovered my weakness when she lived in my house, ate my food, drank my wine, slept in my sheets not fifty feet from the head of my husband. Perhaps it was then that she began to fixate on him, and to rearrange her memory of past events in order to convince herself that he would be her spiritual guide, the essential operator in her life. She needed to spend a lot of time alone with him to find out how.

(25) In a book my enemy gave me I discovered this fact. Let's say there is a quality you are striving for, a quality you consider good. This "positive" quality is one you wish to be identified with and you'd like to believe you have eradicated its opposite from your life. This good quality might be: generosity, wisdom, spiritual transcendence, unselfishness, compassion, or humility perhaps. Take humility. Let's say you want to believe that you are humble. Well, as long as you are in contact with the opposite quality— the opposite in this case being *pride*—that opposite remains dormant in you. And no one, least of all you, can know just when it might erupt.

(26) Many perceptive people have remarked that anger, like all forms of violence, is a sign of weakness. My enemy first made me aware of this fact.

(27) In a recent dream, my enemy stands next to her husband. With the palms of her hands she impassively presses her round full breasts until milk wets the front of her blouse. I look at my husband and see that he, like me, is embarrassed. Hurriedly, her husband explains that they have decided to keep her milk flowing in case their son—age five—ever needs it again. This doesn't make any sense to me. I feel she is trying to be provocative. I am enraged, seeing this as yet another attempt to spark my husband's easily inflamed libido. My mother suddenly appears in front of me, reprimanding, "You've got to throw this whole thing overboard

or you'll drown!"

(28) Muhammad advised that one should give generously of one's self or one's goods, but warned against expecting any reward on this earth.

(29) One day, my enemy gives me another book, this one inscribed —in pencil—"Thank you for everything you have done for me." Later that day she tells me about her dream. In it I am crying, she moves to comfort me as I sit doubled over with anguish. My husband is there also in the dream. He is the one who attracted her attention. He is the one who pointed me out.

(30) We are to meet for lunch at her suggestion. She wants to read the notes I have been collecting in the diary I call *My Enemy*. Why not? I decide to go ahead with it, but only on the condition that she let me pay. I paint my fingernails and wear green eyeshadow. She has spun her long amber hair into a knot and wears an unusually colorful sweater that she says reminds her of Arizona. That settles it, we go to the Vera Cruz . . . with beer and red wine in front of us she reads the diary entries, laughing at all the funny parts. I nervously consider the imagery on the tent card set with the condiments at our place. It's an advertisement for beer from Bogotá: a sturdy young man in an open-necked khaki shirt wields a machete against dense jungle foliage, a toucan rides on his shoulder while a dark-eyed beauty follows wearing a flimsy nightgown. Why are they going into the jungle? What will they find when they get inside? She finishes reading the diary and looks as if she is going to cry. I am not sur-prised. I point out the incongruities in the imagery I have been examining. "One of the daughters of Satan," she advises, "just look at that smile."

Generously then she compliments me; she praises me for my perseverance, my show of integrity these past few years, and my writing style. She is sorry she never said anything before. She can quibble only with one fact in my reckoning of the situation, consideration of which now brings on the tears in full. "There is something you do not understand," she says, and begins to explain certain conditions of her existence I knew nothing about, certain catastrophic occurrences in her life, recent and past, of which I had no cognizance, events in which my husband and I have had no part. This surprises me more than I care to admit. It also saddens and sickens me. There are forces, she asserts, so terrifying, black, and awesome, she can reveal them to no one. She must battle these forces alone—master them all by herself—to capture and cure her being. This is not something she is imagining, I can see that. Her head is tilted, her hands remain open in her lap. I have never seen anyone cry so hard without moving a muscle of the body. Her face, though, is billowing. Rippling and boiling like a waterfall, sparked by the pungent arcs of her solitary ingrown beauty.

(31) As I stand now with my eyes closed thinking of her, it happens. The burning blue becomes red becomes white-hot and is forged into a three-edged sword which loses heat and darkens in the space just in

back of my eyes. As it lengthens—impossibly—driving straight down through the soft parts of my chest and my abdomen, my intestines and my womb, my body resonates with a terrific low sound.

In the evening I ride with my enemy toward the edge of finished earth to a permanent base in the shifting fallopian universe. Here, on a slab of salt and dirt, a handpainted sign marks the spot where gambling first turned to insurance, and the acacia wood ark of the covenant was found. "Where is it now?" I wonder aloud. "Lost to the enemy," she says with a grin. She is making an effort I realize, but catch myself. I ride on alone until I lose interest in thought.

Clayton Eshleman

BAPTIST JOHN

In Caravaggio's late, most tragic painting, before he was murdered in
   Malta, 1610,
Saint John appears to have been struck to the ground. The executioner's
   left arm
is the model for vertical architecture, and in the deltoids and covert biceps
(lit as from the body of a hanged man) I see a sculptural Last Judgement on
   mankind,
this stalagtitic musculature swarms and refolds with sinners,
and the executioner himself is wearing white silk bloomers, as if in the
   swaddling tourniquet
of the monstrous spurt of a baby.   Crewcut executioner, longhair saint.
Night takes up 70% of the painting,   the night of *Nightwood*, the smoky
   brown brick of
the wormwork of the night,   the pulsations of the murderous lords who
coil about our sweating not-innocent bodies and, in an act of mercy,
only extract a bit of semen, or a vial of menstrual dread.

As if figures in a theater,   fixed on a performance,   two prisoners,
forearms reclined on nearly invisible ledge,   behind an iron lattice, tell
me that a woman in Salvador is regarding me here.
In the foreground: the work of the Pentagon,   the war "industry," the
   back-bound wrist-roped
"fugitives,"   people Charlie Clements ascended to—
this is not an allegory,   but a radiating view of man on Man, edifice on
its cornerstoned victim, the glue under the subterfuge, the victim ballast
   that permeates all I know.

Caravaggio was magnetized to beheadings as bull-sharks to Mayan flesh,
the loss of the head,
the loss of the representing cleaner,
our mob-yearn,   this pilot-syllabus,   this spurt-loop we are told
our semen (if we are fellows) yearns to nave up into,
grotto of the sensational explosion of nirvana blotto release secure,
this peak, or metaphoric cowl for a summit,   flu of the soul we are told,
this mirador beached on the labor-deck of the shoulders,

voyeuristic id shaft,   double hole in the fence through which we can glimpse
the team fucking the gleam,   men devouring mastiffs which takes place
under cellophane as part of the basic mooing of being,

could I scream Saint John's bewilderment   his why me   his why me
   whyme   his Whymi
immediately it sounds slimey   and slimey is bad, no?
Caravaggio cheated a bit—put the prison guard (if that is who he is)
in Turkish costume,   allowed no frontal facing of the horror.
But Caravaggio was bigger than his own size:
he could project through his own bilious fortitude a size of world permeat-
   ing beheading.
And the slime of the cry?   The lemon-flavored Adam-cake Eve out of her
   own
bleeding construed,   to build this Exterminator fortress I too lounge in,
my architecture,   I live on the 34th floor of this executioner's arm,
LOOK my son,   I am peeping through a varicosity of trolls and freemen,
as if The Ivory Tower rises from the earth of Baptist John's rape!

And there is no end,   until the singular life   is piss.

The Salome we all inhabit is drugged by the empty baskct.
She rests on its edges,   like elephants rest on Africa,
   in its bosom
         is the flat basin of her morning.

Lisa Bernstein

POEMS

THE WOMAN BETWEEN US

i

She waits, taut as a net,
for me to fall from him,
a torn sail. As if spread on the water,
blanking out, I glimpse
my long brown hair sweeping his shoulder
and dizzy with sunlight
I'm washed back to his shore.
He doesn't see her shape appearing,
a paper lantern outlined
by twine, the curve of her breasts
precise as ink, the down of her belly
brushstrokes of a name.
He reaches for me but her
milky buttocks slope between us,
her body a flicker of lace
flattening as our hips meet
and unfurling as we slip apart.
I cling to his hard, curved chest,
my fingers caught in his red-gold hair,
bite his neck and the flesh
above his ribs. All his weight
can't erase her sheen
from my skin. Open-mouthed,
silent as she is silent,
inhaling with her, exhaling
with him, I cry out—
a white gown unraveling
around me, her heat. We are alone
with her absence. He sees me
transparent, the length of my body
lit up with loving him and
trying to keep her in sight.
He watches me looking
and doesn't look away.

ii

"I was spilled from the glass
you kept by the bed.
Like a man at a drying river
he lapped me up. And offers you
salty mouthfuls from his body,
muscle to lean your cheek against.
His fine hairs like meadow weed
stiffen in the dusk.
His flesh is packed gold clay
and he wants you to draw
where I've already made him soft.

"You lie still, my name sticky
on the sheet, and watch his hands stray
past his ribs fanned with my sweat.
Faithfulness? A stream
that pulses through drought.
The delicate weight of your feet
on the bank, your forearm's arc
as you pointed to me,
knowing he had seen
and looked away.

"Like your shadow on the waves
I will vanish. And reappear
on infrequent days. You grip
your glass of water, suddenly afraid
of its simple taste, your fingers
like a child's, foreshortened and pink.
I'm not yours to hoard anymore,
your quickly drying stain.
You gave him what you thirsted for
and your tongue sweeps his lips for my flavor
of salt and reeds. Your skin,
a surface of blossoms,
hides the current we share beneath.

"Did you want that pull to take him
while he turned in my arms?
To wake him to your sway? He quivers
in your hands, tall and clear: now drink."

iii

In the overlapped shadows
of his body and mine, I reach out
for his muscled thigh, his fingers
which once brushed her waist
now smoothing my skin, gripping
my black hairs—he must close his eyes.
And lie back, the air between us
acute with sadness, as he waits for my body
to cover his, to admit his interrupted
tenderness. His legs wrap my waist,
ankles hooked at the small of my back.
Our fingers part my labia,
guiding him in, our mouths
rounding, every pore in the skin
saying oh. He grimaces,
his daily smile disappears
with each lunge of the hips,
my head thrown back. As her face shimmers
before me, then is gone,
I draw away like an inlet of water
pulling my cold salt weight
from his sand with a sucking sound,
fingers sweeping his shoulder as
sharp as rocks. He tosses his head
to be named and named, a shoreline poised
and overrun. A wind arches
through one body, the other.
His hazel skin against the pillow.
Then I can't turn away from his look
on my lips, breasts, exact as a rope on
my thighs, and hope for a shadow
to twist like a net between us,
crisscross my bare skin.
Her murmur begins: This close
you will lose yourself . . .
I shake my dark curls.
My unseen muscles, pulsing
hold to their taking.
The empty air
rises from our joined hips,
along our slick torsos, a triangle
opening.

THE WISH

He drifts, he's never let himself float
Like this, intangible as a lily bed
as my fingers pass into his torso and grip his ribs—
my hand pulls away, and he's sealed again.
His rosy nipples, his chest hairs a blond net of moss
on the surface of the lake.
Now he lifts himself onto the shore
and I climb out to lie beside him. The water
has shown him how to look me in the face,
healed the red wounds like mouths along his ribs.
He is promising to love me again.
My kiss was like a faint lapping, my gaze
as abstaining as water. He's gone half a year.

In another year, he says, he will see me as I am.
I think of his fingertips on my skin, moistening
with a salt liquid he wouldn't taste
and I stand smiling
as if I were still his wife, as if the lakewater could lift
from the surface and thrash against the mud borders
the miles an ocean hits the sand.
The moon is out. He looks now at my earrings,
pearls he once closed in his hand.
Over his shoulder, the large white circle.
Its pull passes through his torso
and angles into my pelvis, traveling down my legs
into the hard ground.

HIT

A nervous man came to my door, hoping
I'd welcome him in.
He told me of the pain
impinging on him which pried
apart his jaw.
I showed him my bed
and lay next to him
as still as the gray curbs
the cars drove between.
Said I'd lived with a man who

beat down stray sparks
from our sheets, afraid of sudden flames.
The visitor listened
but his eyes kept following
the cars, the small hinge
he saw in the middle of the street getting battered
by the wheels, and it rattled,
the right-angled metal bolted to nothing.

His blue eyes twitched toward my face and
away, watery with the cold.
He started to talk, his hard legs
pinning mine. I kept on smoothing
the sheet. Years ago a child
much older than I
made me sit at her feet. In the chill
she watched the men tarring the roadway
and told me all the times
she'd been beaten. Now in the quiet
I waited for him to say it.
He said Take me—   How do I take you
apart? He saw my small hand
sweeping ashes from the sheets.
He kept talking. His eyes were wet.
I kept watching.

Marilyn Hacker

LETTER FROM GOOSE CREEK: APRIL

for K. J.

We're both in Greenville, but a state apart.
About the time you were due to arrive
I was helping Julie stack wood for the stove.
There was frost last night, when we had to start
the fire up, I remembered you, me, and the dog
sprawled out on the brown and gold rag rug
as you wedged twigs and kindling till the log
caught; then you and I kindled from a hug
while the fire blazed, from slow afternoon's talking.
Bright afternoon here now, through which I drove
two lanes at a journeyman's fifty-five
thirty miles to Goose Creek from the K-Mart
—smooth starts at traffic lights are still the worst part.
What changes nothing changes everything.

There are no detours circumventing grief.
The spare-room pillow's lettered with the "Tracks
Of My Tears" again. I came unstuck
at dawn when grey light off-printed oak-leaf
shapes, vague as clouds before; and then, my eyes
hopelessly open, I pulled last night's clothes
back on. Outside the window, three outsize
woodpeckers in the feeder and a rose-
breasted she-cardinal were bickering
while I rattled round Julie's kitchen, looking for the coffeepot. The falling back's
inevitable. I know you know brief
descents yourself. Juice, coffee, and relief.
What changes nothing changes everything.

You were the friend who got me through the night
I packed her things. It was a few nights after

when, stuck on upper Broadway in your car
with postal sacks you'd ferried me to get,
"Was I a good friend, or an inadequate
lover?" you asked, about our friend, who'd died
with you, months vigilant at her bedside,
years warily defining why and what
you couldn't. Then the wind had you, raging
your mourning across a continent we were
sometimes conjoined by, like the curiouser
fossils. From my stratum, trilobite
dislodged, bordering yours, I did what might
have changed nothing, or changes everything.
Cold rain sheeted the Long Island Expressway
the Ides of March: commuters on our necks.
We were, I noticed, talking about sex
in a half-gossip, half "I should confess . . . " way.
I know I thought, "I wonder where this gets
us, in the rain, stuck indoors on our butts
days, on the edge of nowhere?" I said "Let's"
eventually. Trust me: it took guts
even in the dark, and in the dark, and in the morning,
a new diplomacy to hold the checks
and balances of night, which brought the next
night's badges of courage. I undressed, lay
down with you, until our hands found the best way,
changing nothing, of changing everything.

There isn't question of an instant replay.
The past hasn't sufficiently gone past
for that to be in either's interest.
Still, in the night beside you, I could sleep; stay
sane through a blighted anniversary
walking beside the water in daylight.
I didn't think of her when you touched me,
though she brought my insomnia last night
and in the live oaks is a lingering
absence. While you're being a houseguest
inland, I try, near the Atlantic coast,
something you taught me well enough to keep—see
that something in you touched something in me deeply.
What changes nothing changes everything.

How many states and interstates and cities
will find us, our miles and our trajectories
between us, both maneuvering strange keys

to borrowed rooms? Some universities
will host me, while your wanderlust hosts you
from friend to friend, vistas you never saw
before, to mornings with completely new
prospects, suggesting that you stay or go
on: suddenly an interesting
itinerary on the map of raw
absence. If you weren't young till now,
now's the time. Reading the highways
between the lines, you're geared, you're gone. The key's
what changes. Nothing changes everything.

Julie is reading Cather in the sun.
On our way back, we'll pick up barbecue
to eat with 1982 Margaux
I trucked from home, and fresh collard greens, done
an hour with fatback. (You'd said, "Richer, and heavier"
than what we'd had to drink the night before.
I was pleased you got it right, and cared
to notice such distinctions: a mentor
made shy by pleasure your acknowledging
my map-and-kitchen lore brought me, although
out on the road, the teacher had been you.
I let myself think more bottles of wine
at other road's ends might follow that one.
What changes nothing changes everything.)

This morning I sent you a postcard of
East Carolina University.
You need to learn disponibility.
I yearn to feel I'm central where I love.
That's a difference. Friendships survive, can thrive
on differences. Yours and mine has. Julie and I've
lived ours. A beach walk followed a midday drive.
Sheltered by boulders, with the dog, beside
the Sound in sunlight, you and I made spring
welcome. Because we did, it is today
welcome still, on the live oak trail, while Julie
waits, tanning on a deck chair in the cove.
What's possible is possible: enough
that change is: that one thing changes everything.

Jayne Lyn Stahl

in translation

your blondeness at the top of the stairs
your blondeness parked
by a fragile red car
your blondeness
somehow eludes me.
it works for you like the vague hand
you open to close around mine
your chest alert with ancestral hair.
so much is lost in translation
in transition   how I want to touch you
you'll disappear
into a spain you have known and lost in boyhood
into your travel   the impenetrable
universe the one you keep
locked in your head   in the quiet
under the blondeness I cannot find a name for.
it is incurable this thirst
my tongue on your eyelids
your manliness in another language   one that is foreign
but too familiar.
I wait at the bottom of the stairs
like a nocturnal cat sniffing for dawn
or it is danger I smell while you stand
awake in your blondeness vague
but not false.

Where's Lena?

MARK COOVELIS

Gladstone King told Eddie that blindness comes like a fog, that you can see for a long time while the fog just hangs at the edge of your vision. He said there was a pretty little girl who lived in the house where he was staying when the fog first came, and he called her close to him as often as he could. He squinted at her and said, "Carmen, when you grow up, I want you to marry me." And she laughed like a bunch of bells hanging on a string. King said, "Blindness comes as slow as Jesus, Eddie. In this life nothing happens overnight."

When he knew King, Eddie was having a bad time. He'd left his wife, Lena, and was living alone with his two dogs in a rooming house, upstairs from the old man. He still tended bar and he still slept with the woman who owned the restaurant where he worked.

Those days it was hard for Eddie to fill the hours between waking up and going to work. He usually slept the mornings away, but then he had the long, light afternoons to get through. Sometimes he played basketball with the black guys on the Catholic school playground across the street. The boys called him Geronimo because of the way he looked with his dark hair flying and his dark eyes following the flight of the ball. "Geronimo ah raht," they'd sing, "Geronimo be bad!" Their song made him feel like one of the boys until they broke his nose for him one day. It looked innocent enough, under the boards, everybody going for a rebound in a rough game. But they laughed at the sight of the blood. "Geronimo ain't bad no more."

When Eddie told him about it, King, a black man, laughed too. "You deserve that nose, Eddie," he said. "That's what you get for playing with the big boys."

Most afternoons, Eddie helped the landlady, Mama Jewel, look after King. Eddie's boss and lover, Barbara, told him he possessed two things that made him the perfect companion for a blind man: infinite patience and a decent car. The car, which he had bought when he was first married, was barely running now after eighty-some-odd-thousand miles. And what Barbara called patience was not infinite, though it was hard for anyone to tell—King, Barbara, or Mama Jewel—because Eddie kept quiet.

Then one night, Eddie stopped sleeping with Barbara. The rain started in the late afternoon with fat drops that left marks as big as half dollars on the sidewalk, and by dark it was roaring down. Business at the Depot died down to a handful of regulars, and the waiters sat together near the kitchen drinking coffee. Eddie started drinking early, sharing beers with Ronson, a tall waiter who, when sober, carried himself through the restaurant with the bearing of a race horse. And they kept on drinking after closing time when the waiters were finished cleaning up, and the boys from the kitchen came out to join the fun. Eddie turned the tape player up. It was Lester Young playing "All of Me." Ronson knew the words and sang along. After the song was over, he kept saying, "Take my lips, I'll never use them." The guys all laughed. It was nearly one o'clock before Eddie calmed down and got everybody else calmed down and on their way home so he could close the restaurant. Ronson stayed behind to keep Eddie company. He sat at the bar with his cap on, drinking bourbon now, and watched Eddie wash glasses. "Hey," he said, "there any rooms open in that place you staying?"

"Mama Jewel's place?"

"Yeah."

"I don't know. I'll ask her," Eddie said. "What happened? Denise kick you out?"

"No, man," Ronson said, "I'm just plain gone."

Eddie had finished cleaning up and they were on their way out the door, when the phone rang. Ronson grinned. Then he began to laugh; even drunk he knew who it was.

Eddie answered it. "Hello, Depot."

"What are you doing, Eddie?" It was Barbara, using her boss's voice.

"Closing up."

"It's one. It's after one."

"I had a couple beers with the guys."

"Is everything all right?"

"Everything's fine. It was slow is all."

"I see."

"The rain, you know."

"Yeah, Eddie," she said. Then her voice went soft. "Are you coming over, Eddie?"

Two or three nights a week Eddie closed the restaurant and drove up to the Oakland hills to sleep with Barbara. The first time, about four months ago, was a night like this, raining, dead-slow. Barbara stayed later than usual, after everyone else had gone. She sat at the bar watching Eddie count her money. Playing the bartender, he offered her a drink, lit her cigarette. He watched her head as she leaned toward his lighter. Barbara had a lot of gray hair for a thirty-eight-year-old woman. It flowed away from her part, catching the dim bar light. Eddie'd never slept with a woman with gray hair. It promised something sweet for its very lack of sweetness, like cinnamon.

Barbara waited, sipping vodka, while Eddie went upstairs to put the money in her office. As though he were alone, he went through his whole routine: double checked the kitchen, set the alarms, turned on the night lights, opened the curtains. Barbara watched him. When Eddie was finished, he pulled his hair out of his shirt, and shook it loose. He said, "Finito, bonita."

Outside, the rain had died to a mist. The surface of the parking lot gleamed under the floodlights. Barbara leaned against Eddie and reached in under his jacket. As they kissed, she pressed him against the door of her car. "Follow me," she said. Eddie followed her taillights up the winding roads to her house in the hills. He listened to the radio, rehearsing his story for Lena. He believed she would believe him, so his story was simple. "I went to Brennan's Pub with a couple of guys." In Barbara's yard, rainwater dripped, crackling through the magnolia leaves. In bed, Eddie told her that he'd wanted to sleep with her forever, as her eyes closed with pleasure beneath him, and she whispered, "Oh yes, oh yes, oh yes, oh yes."

"No," Eddie said, "it's late already." The telephone line hummed in his ear.

"All right. See you tomorrow."

"Yeah, see you."

Eddie locked Barbara's restaurant, and wandered down to Brennan's with his new friend through the heavy rain.

And the next afternoon, downstairs in King's room, Eddie said, "I told her no." Eddie stood so close to the old man that he could feel King's breath against his neck. King held his head back, his face raised, one white eye aimed at the place where the wall and ceiling joined. Eddie straightened King's collar and smoothed his lapels.

"What you want," King said, "a medal? Where's my hat?"

Eddie found the hat on the dresser and set it on King's gray cushion of hair. "I'm through being stupid, is all."

"That's good," he said. "That's real fine." King gave the hat a little tug, so that it sat on his head like a gangster's hat and covered his mutilated eye.

They walked together through the cluttered room, the cane tapping against the wall and against Eddie's legs. King stopped at the door and whispered, "Be careful about Mama Jewel, and don't say nothing, hear?" He leaned closer, bitter breath in his whisper. "She say I'm crazy like a child." They tapped their way down the hall. King had gone blind so slowly that he'd refused to use his cane until the last few months before the light faded away. Now he clattered about, an old man, swinging his cane with an awkward and defiant flick of the wrist, as though he were scaring away a dog.

They were gong to Oakland to a downtown pawnshop. King had pawned his trumpet, and now he'd finally put enough aside to pay the balance due; money he'd hoarded from his Social Security checks and refused to give to Mama Jewel for his rent and keep.

Mama Jewel sat by the stove with her short legs propped up on another chair. Her nurse's uniform was unbuttoned, and Eddie could see the top of her bra.

"Lord!" she cried, "y'all going driving 'gin this aftahnoon?"

"I'm taking him to Pay 'n Save," Eddie said.

King stood in the doorway with his head held back, his lips moving up and down as though he were sniffing the kitchen air.

"Ageeyan?" she said.

"He needs some stuff."

"What kind of stuff?"

"Shampoo, mouthwash."

"What else? I got plenty shampoo, if he needs shampoo."

In a low voice, King said, "I need some peppermint candy."

Eddie laughed, and king took hold of his elbow, getting ready to go.

"It ain't good for you, King. You got dyahbeettees, remember?"

"I ain't about to forget about no dyahbeettees, woman."

"Well. What you talking about pep'mint candy then for?"

Eddie said, "It was a joke, Mama Jewel."

"Lord knows, ain't no luck in joking about dyahbeettees."

As though he were talking to himself, King whispered, "I ain't your prisoner."

"What he say?"

"I said I ain't your prisoner, woman."

"No one said nothing about no prison," she whined.

As softly as before, King said, "I can go if I want to go."

"I ain't saying you can't go nowhere."

Without a word, King tapped out at the door space and pulled Eddie along. Slowly, they made their way down the narrow hall. King slapped the walls as hard as he could and worked his jaw around like he always did when he was working up a wad to spit.

Eddie led King across the high, wet lawn to the car and eased him into the passenger seat. King brooded, his head twitching from side to side as Eddie drove down Shattuck to Adeline, past Flint's barbecue and the pink motel. King held his cane with two hands. All of a sudden, he said, "Bah!"

Eddie laughed out loud.

King turned his face toward Eddie. "Bah!" he said, and laughed too. "How she look when I said that about how I ain't her prisoner? How she look?"

"Surprised."

"How surprised? Mad?"

"Hurt more, I guess. Some mad."

"Good. I wish I could've seen. What her mouth do? Did it drop open, like . . . ?" King let his mouth drop open.

Eddie said, "Come on, King, what you want, a medal?"

King moved his hands on his cane, holding it lightly now. He said, "Sometimes, Eddie, you got to be strong."

Eddie didn't feel very strong. He had awakened at noon dry mouthed and heavy headed, thinking about Lena. When he had lived with her, he often woke up to the sound of the shower and then rolled to her side of the bed into her smell and listened, his eyes still closed, to the sounds she made in the bathroom—the click of the medicine cabinet opening and then clicking closed, and the rush of water in the sink—until he drifted back into sleep again. This morning he woke alone. And he couldn't remember whether he'd double checked the kitchen at the Depot or not.

His dogs were scratching at the door, whining. He let them in, and wandered back to the little sink in the corner of his room and leaned over it as though it were a drinking fountain. When he straightened, the water dripped from his chin to his chest, and he remembered being in the Depot kitchen last night, the row of silver knobs on the stove, butterfly-shaped: one, two, three, four, five, six, and the feel of each one closed down tight, off.

In the pawnshop, they heard a police-band radio hiss and sputter somewhere in back. Eddie led King to the counter. King patted his coat and said, "Get the ticket there, Eddie." Eddie found the ticket and pressed it into King's palm. They waited. King tapped his cane on the floor and called, "Hey! Anybody home?"

An old guy with gray hair nearly as long as Eddie's stepped through the blue curtain. "Mr. King, you've returned."

King smiled at being remembered. He said, "What's wrong, you got the police back there?"

The pawnbroker laughed. "No, I just listen for trouble. Long as I know the trouble's out there, I feel safe." He raised his chin toward the window where cars flashed by like the cars of a carnival ride.

King said, "Uh huh," and pushed his ticket toward the old man.

"Oh, yes, Mr. King, you've come for the trumpet."

"I got the money," King said.

"That's fine. Let me see if I can find it, Mr. King."

"You better had find it, Mr. Pawn-man."

They waited. Eddie leaned against the glass-topped counter, and King leaned against him. In the display case beneath Eddie's hand, there was a jumble of watches. The faces he could see were all wrong. They just reminded him that he knew it was twenty to three and that in an hour and a half he'd be at work. At twenty to three he often thought of Lena. She was up at the high school teaching geometry. When they only had one car, he took the dogs and drove up to the school at three o'clock. The three of them, Idaho, Nevada, and Eddie walked against the stream of kids that flowed down the hill toward the busses. The dogs wound their way through the deserted hallways, their collars ringing, until they found Lena's classroom. Later, Lena drove Eddie down to the restaurant during the hour when the headlights of passing cars suddenly flashed on, and by the time they parked behind the Depot, the streetlights glowed in the branches of the city trees.

The man emerged through the blue curtain with the trumpet case in his hands. He placed it on the counter and opened it. The horn lay on the plush blue lining, tarnished as a brass pot.

Eddie held the tall cane, while King took up the trumpet. King worked the keys with a quick, smooth flutter of the fingers, licked his lips, and raised it to his mouth. He blew one short weak note, and put the thing on the counter. He said it sounded fine to him.

"Fine, fine," the salesman said. He pushed a piece of paper at Eddie. "He owes thirty-two, twenty-five."

"What's that?" King said.

"Thirty-two, twenty-five," Eddie said.

King patted himself near his front pants pocket and Eddie reached in for the wallet. He gave a couple twenties to the man. King cocked his head at the sound of the register keys, the drawer slamming open, the bell. The man returned with the change and counted it out on the counter, letting the coins fall, ringing, against the glass. Eddie put everything, including the coins, into King's wallet, and shoved it into the front pocket. King touched himself lightly to see just where it was, as Eddie closed the case and took it up by the handle. King took hold of Eddie's elbow, and they tapped their way toward the door, out of the hiss of the police-band radio and into the world of trouble.

At home in Mama Jewel's kitchen, Eddie stood at the sink washing King's lunch dishes. Through the window, he could see the Catholic girls walking home from school. They walked by, two or three together, in their white blouses, plaid skirts, knee-high socks.

"I'm going to be late, King," he called.

They'd been home for half an hour. Eddie'd fixed King a lunch of boiled franks with mustard and soft bread, a cup of broth, and a cup of red wine. Eddie drank some wine, too. They toasted to the trumpet. Eddie took it out of the case for King to hold. King said the keys felt good and it sure was too bad his teeth were messed up, because he could really play something if his teeth were good. He showed Eddie how the teeth and lips have to work together to get music out of a horn. Eddie puckered up and put the horn to his lips, but nothing happened, not a sound. He tried again, and finally there was a little blast and then a lot of humming noises. All this time King was waiting, a little grin creeping onto his face, until he heard Eddie's one wild note and the sputtering that came afterwards. Then he laughed so hard he spilled his wine on his pants, and Eddie laughed, too, watching him.

Now the dishes were done, and Eddie was alone in the kitchen. He could feel the wine he'd drunk, because time seemed to be passing too quickly.

"Did you hear me, King?"

"Yeah, I heard you, you gonna be late."

Eddie went to King's room. King sat on the edge of his bed. The trumpet lay on the floor at his feet, and the case was open on the dresser. Eddie picked up the trumpet and put it away.

"You always throw your horn on the floor when you were a jazzman, King?"

"No, I never throwed my horn on the floor, and I never had no bad teeth neither, and I sure never had no smart aleck boy calling me a jazzman!"

"It's four, King."

"How you know?"

"The girls are outside."

"You saw them?"

"Uh huh."

"Take off my shoes. I want to sleep some."

Eddie got down on his knees and King lifted his foot. Eddie grabbed the shoe at the heel and pulled it off without untying the laces. Then King lifted the other foot.

"You know what I want?" King said.

"More wine."

"No." King lay down on his bed, one hand touching the wall. "I want a nice-voiced woman. Come here and read to me. Talk. You know, sometimes I hear a woman on the phone and I know she's smiling. I say, You smiling, and she say, How you know that? and I say, It's in your voice like a bell going ding, ding, ding."

The sun was low already in the afternoon, and this side of the house was in shadow, but Eddie hesitated to turn on the light because King would hear the click, and it would tell him that Eddie was staying a little longer. So Eddie just stood there in the gray light.

"Eddie?"

"What?"

"You still there?"

"Yeah, I'm still here."

"Where's the trumpet?"

"I put it in the case on the dresser."

"Let me feel."

Eddie took King by the wrist and laid his hand on the dresser and then on the trumpet case. "See?"

At opening time, Eddie always put the Billie Holiday tape on for good luck, his version of the pawnbroker's police radio.

Ronson sat at a table near the bar folding napkins, lifting the unfolded ones from the chair next to him, and folding them on the table. He stopped folding, tapped a Camel from his pack, and held it for a few moments in the candle flame. His long black fingers toyed with the unfiltered cigarette as though it were a joint. He took a drag and started in on his napkins again. Suddenly, the side door opened with a rattle of keys; the lights from the parking lot shined in. Barbara's silhouette passed through the door space and moved past the table where Ronson sat. She stopped and turned and looked down at him as though surprised to see him. He looked up at her through his cigarette smoke. His face was already the mask of calm that he'd perfected for moments like this. "Come upstairs," she said, and turned toward the bar. "Eddie, bring me a cup of coffee."

Eddie heard the jangle of keys as she opened her office door and then a crash as her key ring landed on her desk. Ronson carefully placed his cigarette in the ash tray and looked at him. He grinned. Eddie made Barbara's coffee the way she liked it, two sugars and milk, and led the way upstairs.

"Did you go home last night?" Barbara asked. Today Barbara wore no makeup and Eddie could see the fine pattern of veins in her cheeks. She had a three-day cycle with her makeup, two days with, one day without, like she couldn't quite decide whether she needed it or not.

Ronson folded his arms across his chest and didn't say anything.

"I've been talking to Denise," Barbara said. "She says she's going to kill you."

Ronson laughed out loud.

Barbara took a sip of her coffee. Eddie leaned against the door, his hand on the doorknob. He turned it back and forth.

"I think she means it," Barbara said.

"She's crazy."

"She says you haven't been home in a week."

"I've been home."

"Well, she says she's coming here tonight."

"Bitch better not," Ronson said.

Barbara smiled her big smile at Ronson, and then over his shoulder at Eddie. "With a knife. I thought you should know."

"It ain't your problem," he said. "I'll handle it."

Barbara put both hands flat on her desk. "In my restaurant it's my problem. When she comes, go in the kitchen. I'll talk to her first. Or Eddie will." She looked at Eddie, then let her eyes fall closed. He opened the door for Ronson to leave.

"Fine," Ronson said.

When they were alone, Barbara said, "You talk to her. I talked to her all day." She pushed her hair behind her ear and sat back in her chair. She had tiny ears pressed to the side of her head. "So, what happened?"

"I left him at Brennan's."

"And what happened to you?"

"I was tired. I'd been drinking. I didn't want to come to you all drunk."

Barbara toyed with the keys on her key ring. "All right, all right. That's good. Don't drink tonight, then. You're supposed to be working, anyway."

"I'll talk to her, if you want."

Barbara said, "I want."

Ronson stood at the window looking over the curtain rod. "She's here," he said. And there she was, at the bus stop across the street, watching the restaurant door. It was quite dark now, but Eddie could see her in the streetlight, her straightened hair falling and blowing across her face. He went outside and met her on the sidewalk.

"Ronson in there?" Denise's head was lowered and she looked up at Eddie sideways, like a boxer.

"Come around back, and he'll come out." He told her to wait by the back door and went inside.

Ronson leaned against the bar, holding a pack of cigarettes in his hand.

"She's waiting for you," Eddie said.

Ronson tapped his cigarette pack against his palm.

Barbara asked, "What's she look like?"

"Barb, I can deal with it," Ronson said.

She looked at Eddie. "Is she under control?"

He shrugged. "She's just standing there."

"I know what she wants," Ronson said.

"You go with him, Eddie, and make sure everything's all right."

Outside, in the light from the street and from headlights swinging in smooth and random arcs, Denise waited, leaning against the restaurant wall. Ronson walked straight up to her.

"Give me my money, Ron."

Ronson reached into his front pocket and pulled out a roll of bills. He dropped it in her hand without even looking at it. He just watched her face, the pout on her lips, in her eyes. Then he looked out across the parking lot toward the traffic at the stoplight. A dog barked. In the distance there was the high, sweet, chilling sound of a siren. "I'll talk to you tonight," he said.

"Bullshit." She turned on her high heels and made her way between the cars in the lot.

Ronson watched her go, his face mask-like under the floodlights. "It's business, Eddie. Fucking dollars and cents."

At closing time, Barbara was at home waiting for Eddie, and Ronson was the last waiter working. He came to the bar and leaned into the candle flame to light a cigarette. "You can pour me a cold one. I'm done."

Eddie poured him the beer. "Hard night?"

"Shit yeah, hard."

Ronson pulled a tangled wad of bills out of his pocket and set it on the bar. Snapping and smoothing each bill, he made three stacks of twenty. Then he counted each stack again with a quick, smooth flick of the wrist, like a bank teller. "I worked too hard for sixty shitty dollars tonight. It ain't right. It's a goddamn curse."

Eddie poured himself a beer. "Waiter's curse," he said. "Bad tips."

"It's Denise. She's ruining my concentration. She's all the time getting on me about all this crap I gotta do. More money. A real job. A car. Until I go crazy."

Eddie burned across the shoulders and down his legs. He was dead tired, but he knew he wouldn't sleep. This was his curse. There was a time when he could sleep after making love with Lena. But then drinking became easier, and he curled up with his back to her, enveloped in the warmth of four vodkas, and pretended to sleep until sleep came. And then for a while, Barbara put him to sleep. That's what he remembered best about the first night with her, the sweet sleep in her strange bed. He didn't want to listen to Ronson's complaints.

"Yeah, all right, okay Ronson. Let's close this dump down and get out of here."

"You going up to the boss lady's?"

"Finito," Eddie said. "No mas."

"Good for you, home boy. How 'bout a ride?"

"Yeah, I'll give you a ride home."

"I ain't going home."

Eddie drove up Grand Avenue to the liquor store, where Ronson jumped out and bought a bottle of Ten High bourbon and more Camels, and then onto the freeway and off again into the dark streets near the factories to a converted warehouse called Michael's Place. Ronson knew some people with coke. Eddie sat at the bar watching people dance under the flickering lights. Ronson disappeared into the men's room with a blonde, faded, pretty woman who reminded Eddie of Barbara. While he waited, he ordered a barbequed chicken to go. In the quiet moment after the music stopped and before the voices rose up, the woman returned to the bar. And then Ronson appeared with the cocaine, happy at last.

In Mama Jewel's kitchen, Ronson leaned back in a straight backed chair with his head against the blue flowered wallpaper. He talked and Eddie listened. His voice seemed to sing with the cocaine and bourbon, deep and rhythmic. Eddie heard with a rare clarity, as though the words hadn't traveled through air, but had risen to his ears along the flesh of his neck.

Ronson said that the preachers were right and the world was going to burn in the end like Hiroshima and that he had a woman in New Orleans who was rich and long-legged, who had seen flying saucers off the Gulf Coast disturbing the water like a storm. He said that women knew things that men would never know because they were tuned into the cycles of the moon like the sea itself. He knew a woman once who jumped off the Golden Gate Bridge on a full moon because her man had gone back to Atlanta with her sister. Women were a curse like the Bible said, and even a white woman he lived with once in Chicago was crazy and couldn't stop crying for more than two hours at a time. The Chicago Seven were betrayed by a woman who worked for the F.B.I. Every great man was ruined by a woman. Look at Huey Newton. Look at the way Denise was acting in front of strangers. Look at movie stars. He said none of this really mattered to him because he was going to buy a bass and learn to play it and join a band. He used to do background vocals in New Orleans. He knew his music. Anyway, his brother in Chicago had lots of cash, but he wanted to keep it a secret about the source. A mystery. The only secret worth keeping in the world except where to get good cocaine at two in the morning. He said his mother was Puerto Rican, spoke with an accent, and still looked thirty-five. He wished he had an accent because women fall for accents on black dudes. You have to be special, he said, because the world is running down. Look at the restaurant. Run by a woman and doomed to fail because women are blind in a man's world and only feel the way the earth moves with some kind of sense they have in their center, their womb, that fills them with fear and makes them cry like that woman he knew in Chicago. But cocaine was something wonderful, and as long as it was around he didn't worry about what women cried about or even if Denise thought she could come into the restaurant he worked in and act crazy. Preachers'll be right in the end no matter what happens and women know it more than men ever will. That's why they sing in choirs so good and sell their bodies on the street, jump off bridges, cry, and do stuff like Denise did. It's all tied to this thing called hysteria, he said. Only women get it, and most men don't understand it like he understood it. It is a forewarning of doom and preachers understand it because they're like women being close to God and all. But white boys never even get a clue, he said, and Eddie sure was lucky to have Ronson for a friend because wisdom of this kind was hard to come by.

Ronson hardly ceased talking long enough to breathe. He talked even while cutting his lines, leaning in over the mirror, using all of the harsh kitchen light to see by, still talking away.

The cocaine shimmered like light in Eddie's head. He wanted to talk. Talk about Lena and love and the mess he'd made of everything. About King and his trumpet and his wish for a woman to come talk sweetly to him.

He looked at Ronson sitting in front of the blue-flowered wallpaper. The sack of barbeque lay on the table between them untouched. Their glasses had about an inch of bourbon in them. Ronson's face caught the kitchen light, his cheeks and forehead shining silver. When Eddie spoke, he said, "I bet you I can tell you the time. Exactly."

The clock was on the wall behind Eddie. Ronson looked up at it.

Eddie said, "It's four-forty-five in the morning."

When he opened his eyes, it was almost two in the afternoon. He didn't feel as though he'd slept at all. His legs burned, his face was moist with sweat, and there was a burning sensation in his chest like an urge to weep. He lay in a bar of sunlight; the sheets were hot to the touch. He looked out the window at the smooth, cream-colored wall across the way. Then he heard King. A short blast from the horn drifted up from downstairs. And then another, lower in tone, and another. He wanted to take a shower to get the stink off, to cool the burning sensation across his shoulders. But he just lay there watching the wall next door, listening to King's trumpet.

After his shower, he dressed in clean clothes. He shaved. He brushed his hair until it was wild with static and tied it back tightly. He wanted everything to be clean and in order. He made his bed. In the kitchen, the dogs had torn into the barbeque bags and spread the bones and paper all over the floor. They lay together under the table by the radiator watching him gather up the mess. Idaho, the black and white Brittany Spaniel, ventured out first and rubbed against Eddie's leg. Nevada, the liver-colored mut, put his muzzle to his paws. Eddie turned to him and said something that he often used to say when he was married and he wanted his dogs to come to life. He said, "Where's Lena?"

Nevada rose from beneath the table, his tail high, and bounded for the door. He sniffed along the bottom edge and turned in circles, whining. Idaho jumped, his front paws landing on Eddie's thigh. And this small pain was enough. Eddie cried. He put his face in his hands and wept, and let himself weep until it was over. The ache rolled up and down in the back of his throat, his face contorted. Exhausted, he cupped his hands under the tap and laid his face into the cold water. With his face still dripping, he went into the living room to wake Ronson. Ronson was asleep on the couch, fully clothed, without a blanket. Eddie said, "Rise and shine, man, you're gonna be late."

At the high school, Eddie drove up the long driveway past the blue and white busses. Down the hill, kids were finding seats in the grandstand, and the lights above the football field were shining dully against a stone-blue sky. He let the dogs out of the car, and took up the short stick he kept in the back seat. They walked through the crowd of kids, Eddie tapping his stick against his leg as he went. Idaho and Nevada followed him, undistracted by the rush of bodies heading toward the grandstand and busses. Near the building, there were fewer students, and the dogs moved ahead into the quiet halls. Eddie walked, tapping his stick, hearing the sound of his own footsteps echoing, and the crackling of the dogs' eight paws on the tiles.

Lena's classroom was empty. For a moment, Eddie hoped he was in the wrong room, but the dogs grew excited by Lena's familiar smell. They slid toward her desk on the smooth floor and sniffed around her chair. Eddie stood in the doorway holding his stick in two hands. The blackboard was covered with geometry—triangles, circles, cubes, numbers. It was all a confusion to Eddie. The only thing he understood were the two words written neatly in Lena's school-teacher handwriting: Given and Thus.

He called the dogs. He hoped to catch Lena in the parking lot. Running through the empty hallways, Eddie felt his strength welling up. When he got outside, he slowed down to a trot. He felt at ease, and stopped running. He didn't have to run. He knew he'd find her, tonight, tomorrow, soon.

Eddie led the dogs down the stairs toward the gym. It was almost dark now. He watched the dogs take the steps, their ears bouncing. He opened the gate to the tennis courts, and still felt the cold of it on his hand as he walked across the empty courts to the next gate. He emerged on a service road that led to the deserted baseball field. The chainlink backstop shimmered like a web before the dark trees, and the dusk light made the dirt of the infield glow, silvery. Beyond the centerfield fence the football game had started, and the sound of the crowd rolled toward him in waves.

"Idaho," he whispered. The dog stood still, watching him. Eddie threw the stick, and the dog jumped after it, running with his ears back, into the grass. The dog came back, trotting, the stick in his mouth. Eddie took it, and yelled, "Nevada!" as loudly as he could, hurling the stick into the dark beyond second base. Nevada ran after it, and Idaho stood beside Eddie, open mouthed, breathing. Eddie waited for Nevada, thinking that he wanted to stand out there forever hurling that stick into the dark. He wanted to yell those names and hear his voice in his ears for one second and hear it disappear into silence. Nevada came back and dropped the stick at his feet. He picked it up, and with all his strength he threw it out into the dark field, calling, "Iidaahoo!"

Karen Finley

PANIC ATTACKS

Mother, do you have a prick?

Yes, I do. Just like cows do.

After my mother washed me, powdered me, I insisted that
she masturbate me.
You wonder why I have panic attacks.
You dreamed you ate me through my silken panties.
But you've got it wrong. I don't smile when I come.

When we go on vacation we stay at the Kon Tiki Motel. They decorate
with a turquoise Pacific Island motif. And, of course, orange telephones.
People were fucking all around us. Upstairs, downstairs, next door and
down the hall. Short fast bangs. Motel beds screwed in the walls banging.
We didn't fuck like that at home. We didn't fuck—instead we'd walk
around our room puffing on Belairs listening to the fuck sounds. All of the
lights would be off except for the glow of the neon Kon Tiki sign illuminating our exhaling smoke.
It was very romantic. Then we'd sneak down to the lobby to the grass hut
lounge Shipwrecked and match faces with the heard fuck sounds as we
sipped drinks the color of sea foam, marshmallow and toast.

He loved to wear silk knotted scarves around his neck.
He'd finger, stroke the silken knot with his long fingers.
He sold silk scarves at a Madison Avenue boutique. I'd watch him for
hours as he sold hankies and neckties to strangers. It gives me great pleasure to watch strangers touching. I'd imagine him masturbating me with
his silk scarves. The scarf would be twisted around me like a long lock of
hair. Very slowly he would move the silk along my crack. Just as I am
about to come he performs a magic trick on me—he'd pull an oiled knotted scarf out of my asshole. I'd fall to my knees on Bloomingdale's floor
and pick up invisible change as I looked up shoppers' skirts.
In the thrift shop in Old Phoenix we found a lamp, a chandelier actually
made of egg cartons and marbles. We didn't buy it but instead we bought a
circular handmade doily with pink rosebuds on the edges. The rosebuds
make me think of erect nipples. I love men who like to have their nipples
sucked.

©1988 by Dona Ann McAdams

The cashier at the thrift shop kept a rock in a clear glass jar immersed in water, level with his ears. When I asked him about the rock—out of no-where appeared stones and crystals and gems and minerals from pockets and wrists were emptied of slivers of slate, pebbles out of Lucky Strike packets. Large lithics, pale lumps of olive and dawn-colored earth.
Yes, he collected rocks.
He also buried the rocks in faraway parts of the desert.
I thought he was returning the specimens back to the Earth.
Isn't that heroic? He was burying the minerals for safekeeping. "You never know when you would need a part of the World" he told me in secret.
"One does not know such things" I agreed.
He had been a doctor once.
I'm sure he was a good doctor.
"He didn't have psoriasis. He's just turning into one big piece of coral," an elderly citizen of Phoenix said. I didn't ask him why he was a cashier in a thrift shop now when he had once been a doctor cause you never know what happens to one's life. You just never know.
That's why I say "WHATEVER GETS YOU UP IN THE MORNING! Whatever, whatever gets you up in the morning."

So, when people ask you—
Why do you spend so much money on rent?
Why do you spend so much time in the clubs?
Why do you spend so much money on clothes?
Why do you always take taxis and never the bus?
Why do you live in such a bad neighborhood?
Why do you drink all the time?
Why do you only spend time with your friends and not your family?
You just look'em straight in the eye and say:
cause it makes me happy—
cause I get a kick out of it—
cause I enjoy my life not like you—always saving—living a boring, cheap ungenerous lifestyle for a future that'll never be.
See, the next time when you visit your family and they say,
How can you live like that?
Just look at 'em straight in the eye and say
EASILY!   Just as long as it's as far away as possible from you!
I'm giving my life everything that you didn't give me.
—FUN—PLEASURE—LOVE WITHOUT CONDITIONS
Generosity and Helping others.

Either go home with the attitude that as an artist this is good material or just don't go.

Photograph by Tricia Pistay

La Loca

from

ADVENTURES

Hello, animal sacrifice hotline?
Do you incinerate teenage boys?
Here they come
The Swarm
Hear the drone of their skateboards
As they approach
like an armada
and run
for cover of the nearest sleazy bar
where they check i.d.
and have bouncers like rhinoceri
Secrete thyself on the furthest stool
Shield thyself with a vodka martini
and wait till the air raid siren ceases.

17 years ago
polite company
screwed on hallucinogens
with the intent to produce
offspring which would be
trippy.
This coup of genetic engineering
enacted at be-ins under bushes on acid
was to be the Aquarian gift to the race.
After all, by 1961
God's remains had been discovered in a
tar pit by the County Museum.
He was dead.
Laboratories were Lord
and Chemistry was Life.
Junkies and alkies slouched the earth
Supreme.
And the brain-damaged naturally selected the
brain-damaged
and they were born
incubated on fungus and fry
yanked from the host
buzzed like a saw.
The Scions of Altered Consciousness.
The New Breed.
And now
the population is overrun with the little
aberrations.
And the little aberrations are so huge.
Bigger than me.
Dinosaurian!
Come to find out
Pre-natal dosages of
lysergic and tetrahydrocannabinol
induce giantism and
increased production of androgen
and here they come again
The Master Race
Flowing in a fleet
a platoon
the hellish sibilance of metal crushing concrete
and
The pack veering toward me in formation
like I'm quarry.
I'll just keep walking down the sidewalk

like I don't notice
the juggernaut of testosterone
mowing me down.
I grip my purse to me, tight
with the angst that only those in
majority can know and
I pray to the God who was re-instated
in 1979:
Please
let this be the primarily peyote-gestated branch
which rarely bites
Please
let them be crocked on
popsicles, Coors and cheap Mexican weed
Please, please
just let me get to the end of the block
without getting a chunk of my butt
tweaked by a twit
and they thrash by
thunderous
in a deafening brouhaha
with a mighty "fuck this" and
a mighty "fuck that"
Fuck biology
Fuck trigonometry
Fuck those PDAP meetings my old man makes me go to
Fuck the cops
Fuck Reagan
Fuck Deukmajian
Fuck Felicia that trendy twat with her fat-assed sister
Fuck Madonna
Fuck Heavy Metallers
Fuck Death Rockers
Fuck Punks
Fuck Trendies
Fuck Stoners
Fuck everybody everywhere in the entire world
all the time for any reason.
A congested aggregate of gnats
dense with fuck
and they slalom around me
and I only get goosed once.
Thank you God.
There is a God.
I take a deep breath.
. . . .

Bernadette Mayer

NO NUKES

Here swig from this rain barrel, a real beautiful candle takes place in the air, I am swimming in the murmuring curtains I take a chance with, not so bent as you fresh vegetables though I bend around

Thanks thank you or vice versa there is a calm time in the poor heart of human tooth hurts without instrument of metal of elements irradiate none such did exist sweet tea thee thine and a practical caring for the sheep!

Little babies so noisome I mean noisy & nosy suddenly I didn't get to see everything as decrepit distracted food-maker in full moon no fun

Bits of that now the morning lake how it be darling I am ever till I be die so what another's same as me be animal or cover even pillow in woods darker citier dictionary of smashed philosophy

Put hand on born & be in a box with me damn me as a darning needle to ever be anything non but noncombustible and noncommercial, look 'em up in your dictionary, I'll be all-Nons, page 997 to page 1000, nonabsorbent to nonyielding

Difficult sweet my brother Non, the time is yielding as is the old bending bed, my sister nonseditiously come into it with me, in other languages said differently, what a little nonvestibular life we could lead

If we could get over our nonvenomous nonvenous & nonverminous ways back past the nonvertical nonvernacular amidst the nonviable nonvesiculae nonvibratory & nonvicarious nonviolation

Of the great hope of living in a nonvirulent & perhaps nonvisiting way not with the nonvisual & nonvocal though, I am nonspottable too, the spotted touch me not man or woman sex parts of all nontarnishable time

Don't come near me the sheen of the length of my idiotic hair so nonsecular, all the nons!

Nonabstainer, nonacceptance, nonadjectival, nonaesthetic, nonaggressive, nonalcoholic, nonallegorical, nonalphabetic, non-American, nonappearing, nonaquatic, non-Aryan, nonassociable, nonauthoritative, nonautomotive, nonbeliever, nonbelligerent, nonblooming, non-Buddhist, nonbudding, nonbusiness, noncaking, non-Catholic, noncelestial, noncensored, nonchargeable, nonchemical, non-Christian, nonchurch

Noncivilized, nonclinical, noncoercive, noncognitive, noncohesive, noncollaborative, noncollapsible, noncommercial, noncommunicating, noncomplying, nonconciliating, nonconservative, noncontiguous, nonconvertible, noncreative, noncrucial, noncrystalline, nondefensive, nondefining, nondehiscent, nondependence, nondetachable, nondidactic, nondisfranchised, nondivergent

Nonedible, nonemotional, nonequal, nonerotic, nonexotic, nonexplosive, nonexternal, nonextraneous, nonfading, nonfanciful, nonfatal, nonfertile, nonfictional, nonfigurative, nonfireproof, nonflowering, nonflowing, nonflying, nonfreezing, nongelatinous, nongenerative

Non-Greek, nongregarious, nonhabitable, nonhedonistic, nonhistoric, nonhostile, nonhuman, nonhumorous, nonidentical, nonidiomatic, nonimaginary, nonimperial, non-Indian, non-Indo-European, noninfinite, noninjurious, nonintercourse, nonintersecting, nonintoxicant, non-Irish, non-Latin, nonliterary, nonlocal, nonluminous, nonlustrous, nonmarital, nonmaritime, nonmarriageable, nonmarrying, nonmartial, nonmaterial, nonmaternal, nonmember, nonmimetic, nonmobile

Nonmortal, nonmystical, nonmythical, nonnative, nonnatural, nonnaval, nonnecessity, non-Norse, nonobedience, nonodorous, nonpacific, nonpagan, nonpapal, nonparental, nonperceptual, nonphilosophical, nonpoetic, nonpolarizable, nonprepositional, nonproducer, nonprofiteering, nonprolific, non-Prussian, nonpsychia, nonracial

Nonreality, nonrecoverable, nonregenerating, nonreigning, nonreprehensible, nonresidual, nonresonant, nonrestricted, nonrevolving, nonrhyming, nonrhythmic, nonrigid, nonritualistic, nonrival, nonroyal, nonruminant, nonsacrificial, nonscientific, nonscoring, nonseasonal, nonsecretory, nonsensitized, nonservile, nonshattering, nonsmoker, nonsocial, nonsovereign, nonspeculative, nonspherical, nonspottable, nonstretchable, nonsubmissive

Non-Swiss, nonsyntactic, nontaxable, nonteachable, nontestamentary, nontheatrical, nontheological, nontherapeutic, nontitular, nontoxic, nontragic, nontropical, non-Turkish, nonuniversal, nonuser

Nonvolatile, nonvolcanic, nonvoluntary, nonvoting, nonvulcanizable, nonworker, nonyielding

Then the fat ape is a care car nonnuclear
It's ten even here over the mushroom cloud
It's a bite, a lot, go to it military men!
Horn tool baby look oil! Be greedy!
Out up use fur maybe or cluster bombs
Get joy yet but how?
Chins & she he thin & then, gone
Leisure rings for ago no bombs then

Agent sanity complies in focus
All words do as in able
Oh heart oh fire coeur feu
Monday morning coq au vin
The duc de France — ich! doch!
This is hypothetical
Dreamed up
& derived from something
Sweet the beautiful flowering somethings
That do it's true turn my attention
Away from you my destruction

Outside are the ape cars
By which we witches make dinner
Inside the secret boiling turmoil
Of the periodic vagina! Lovely!
How defensible! There is a little
Man who is a woman and with her
We make gold eggs & balls
Maybe to sell at great cost who knows

Or to threaten the enemy with
When the sulphur is dried
Like milfoil on the most real dock
The sincere pier of a not nonidiotic god
Heart and nonrhyming of a nonhim
All cooking and fucking and serving
Maiden pink spoons for the dinner
Coated with the deadly nightshade
To touch the tongues of those who eat.

Meat

ROY SCHNEIDER

Jazz in the mirror, locked on himself. The hard line of a young man's jaw: a lie. Grins at the stench of caged souls, unbathed and aroused. Breathes in the details.

"Let'em know it ain't no problem." His smile only slightly reptilian. "Rough'em up from the nipples down. You know, bang'em 'til they bruise."

He's drifting in the demon's breath. A stench thick as the blood in the trees. Dreams of willows that bleed when broken. He's seen the stuff himself. Soft pouches of thawed afterbirth his mother used for fertilizer. Earth that gives off his scent.

Lover behind him, sprawled on stiff sheets. Broad arms carrying the tattoos of two continents. Blue serpents blurred with age, but muscle still thick on the bone.

"You lyin' again, baby . . . but it sure is sweet."

He stares from the bunk, pale eyes stuck on a ceiling that never goes dark. The lid of this cell: freedom defined.

"Keep it comin', boy. C'mon, give me somethin' that's gonna moisten up these dreams."

There's a throb in the head. The rhythm of meat loose in the breast. A hum slowly gaining speed, pressure. Echoes of dead lives in storage. Caged souls and steel. Leaves nothing but skull-shining fear and the taut metallic bite of a barbed-wire gag. Cool strands, ear to ear. And the hum, building.

Now he hears his own words, feels their distance, and turns.

"Hey, this one's so good you won't have to put your hands in your pockets for a week."

The mention of the word "mother" is anxiety provoking as evidenced by his masturbation during sessions. In a five-year-old child, such behavior in the presence of adults is usually inhibited, but he has a striking eroticism unusual for a child his age. This is displayed by his use of dark colors, phallic and feminine forms in his drawings, and a smile that is slightly reptilian.

"It was a sweet accident . . . just a burglary. I mean, I was coming down a little hallway, something like this, and the bathroom door opens and she steps out. I covered her with the gun . . . told her not to make any noise . . . just keep it quiet. And she said, 'What do you want?' And I told her I was going to rob her and I wanted money. And she said, 'I don't have

very much.' And she was naked . . . just got out of the shower, I guess. And, shit, me just creepin' in the hallway."

We saw him slip the paper from his pocket, start writing. Paid no attention to us. Just wrote. Only a moment of words. When he left, she pulled it from the trash, handed it to me.
"From dad," she said.
A single line: "If they're old enough to bleed, they're old enough to butcher."

"I told her, 'C'mon, baby, I'm gonna tie you up.' So I took her into the bedroom and she sat on the bed. And I couldn't find anything that looked real good, you know, for tying her up. Then I saw the curtain cords hanging down. So I told her I needed a knife . . . She took me into the kitchen. I was following, just keying on that ass . . . middleaged, but still sweet. I just watched it quiver . . . the shit dancing right there cock-high . . . used but not abused. She shoulda had on high heels, put it on a pedestal.
". . . She gave me a steak knife."

He was mad when the two men started kissing her. They knew he was watching. One was lying on top of her, caressing. I asked if they were naked. He said, "yes" and described how they touched each other all over. He again said that he was very angry. I asked if the people touched him and he said, "Mommy made me." He said it felt strange. He said the men also touched him and his mother touched him . . . It was around Christmastime.

"So, I'm thinkin' about that sweetness right. Gettin' lost in that soft ass . . . I took her back in the bedroom and cut the cords down and tied her up. And I started going through the house . . . there was some money. Maybe fifty, sixty dollars. I couldn't find anything else, so I thought, 'Leave, man.' . . . Just a burglary, right? Really, I thought about it . . . but then I said, no, no. She was looking pretty good laying there. And I thought, well, I might as well go ahead and get a piece of ass while I'm at it. You know, since I'm stealing things, I might as well steal some of that, too."
"So I took my clothes off and got on the bed with her . . . started rubbing her up . . . whatever I wanted. And at first she was just kinda laying there. And I told her she better make it a little better than that if she expects to get through it. And she started saying shit like that if you kill me you won't get anything . . . Tied up and talking shit! So I told her, 'Hey, I'll go ahead and get it anyway, bitch. Dead or alive?' She just kept laying there. Wouldn't do anything . . . I rolled her over and tore into that brown eye."

At points, while talking, he has expressed explicitly that he doesn't miss the mother nor does he wish to see her again.

"When I got through, I tied her feet back together again and I was still trying to figure out what I could do. I had on gloves. And the only thing I could think of was kill her, strangle her. I didn't want to shoot her 'cause it made too much fuck'n noise. And I didn't really want to stab her 'cause it's messy. So I got another piece of cord and started choking her. And it seemed like it was taking forever. You know, limp but not dead. So I took the knife and think I'll just cut her throat, right? . . . But I didn't slice it. I just kinda jabbed at it a few times . . . shit, almost tender . . . and she started cryin' and shakin' and I told her, I said, 'Ain't no need to cry.' And I thought, well, you know, maybe if I could just pork her again she'll calm down.

Remember: slide it in to the first knuckle, and wait. When the smile comes, ease in full fingers, look for the nod. When the lips are taut and the eyes say go, punch through to the wrist, relax in the musky smell of grief. Watch the eyes. When they ease back into the head, go to mid-forearm, and wait. When he comes, loosen the ligature, start his breathing again. And give a false address.

"So, damn . . . she's a mess, some blood and shit. But I rolled her over again and started in. And I'm tellin' you, she ain't fighting it too hard . . . she's wet. But she was still only going at it about half assed. So I said, C'mon, bitch, I think you can do better.' And she's cryin' and she says 'Well, that's why my husband left me.' Weird shit like that! Crying about this guy walking out! She said he left a little note—'I'm gone. I'm outta here. I'm sorry.' . . . Man, I didn't want to hear that shit!"

We all took off our clothes inside the house and went outside to the back yard. The men were taking pictures of us. Mommy was sitting like an Indian. She said, "Put your hand inside me." It was wet. She laid down and had her legs straight out and I lay on her.
She said, "Honey, let's make babies."

"Yeah, well, I got my rocks off again. The bitch couldn't stop that. And I got up and I figured, shit, that's rape. She's gonna call the cops. I said, 'Well, I'm gonna have to kill you, babe.' . . . Shit, I knew I was gonna kill her. Ain't no burglary now . . . And I started to choke her with a piece of the cord. Thin shit though, wasn't doin' the job so good . . . So I stabbed her in the back a few times . . . I don't know . . . two or three. One time I hit bone and she made a funny noise. And she kinda relaxed, like she was dying.

"But I didn't know if she was faking it. So I picked up the knife and gave it one more try.

" . . . nailed a tit to her heart with both hands."

A shift in the bed sends it in motion. Beefy hands through a young man's hair. Thick lips on soft ears. Warm words hang in silence, aroused.

"Honey, you such a cold mother if we store meat up your ass it'd never spoil."

The eyes don't meet. A whisper, the noise of choice.

"Yeah, but the weirdest shit, man, was that I remember when I was leaving, it looked like her hair was coming off . . . just a slab of skinned meat . . . I mean, I didn't know whether she was wearing a wig or what. Looked like she was baldheaded or something . . .

I dunno . . .

What do you think?"

Drawing by Fred Wickham

from

AUTOGEDDON
A Handbook for Car Haters and Lovers

HEATHCOTE WILLIAMS

If an Alien Visitor were to hover a few hundred yards above the planet
It could be forgiven for thinking
That cars were the dominant life form,
And that human beings were a kind of ambulatory fuel cell:
Injected when the car wished to move off,
And ejected when they were spent.

In 1885 Karl Benz constructed the first automobile.
It had three wheels, like a car for invalids,
And ran on alcohol, like many drivers.

Since then about seventeen million people have been killed by them
In an undeclared war,
And the whole of the rest of the world is in danger of being run over
Due to squabbles about their oil.

If the Visitor's curiosity was still aroused on landing,
It would soon discover
From hoardings, newspapers and television advertisements,
That the car appeared to satisfy a compendious spectrum of desires:
Sexual, social, economic, political and religious . . .
And that it had as much to do with getting from A to Z
As with getting from A to B—

'Drive it like you hate it'   Volvo.
Car as enemy. But an enemy that only you can control.

'Step on the Exhilarator'   Datsun.
Car as marital aid.

'Believe in freedom. Believe in Honda.'
Car as Universal Declaration of Human Rights,
Drafted with you alone in mind.

'Nothing performs like a Saab.'
Car as harlot.

'Kiss the old ideas goodbye.'   BMW.
Car as radical chic.

*'Nothing else quite so perfectly reflects
one's achievements in life.'*   Daimler.

A car that gives you permanent positive feedback
And insulates you from any other.

If any customer seems to be choking,
Mercedes steps in with the sleek and recherché invitation
To *'Experience more breathing space . . . '*
Though their motivational analysts would be loathe to admit
That many cars
Prevent both customers, and complete strangers,
From breathing for a long, long time.

The accessories, the spare parts,
Known in the trade as the 'fluff,'
Are not to be overlooked:
Dunlop peddles *'A Tire That Saves Gas!'* It thriftily explodes.
Pirelli Tires hustle their wares with giant photographic blowups
    of tire-tread
Captioned *'The Basic Pattern of Life,'*
Their tires will plumb the mysteries of evolution,
While doubling as rubber time bombs
And bringing primeval chaos bang up to date.

The Alien Visitor steels himself for a closer look:
Their owners are washing them, caressing them,
Polishing them and petting them
As if they were a member of the family—
A scratch on the body draws the same fury reserved for child-molesters . . .
Techno-tom-cats spraying the boundaries of their inviolate territory,
They mark out their vehicles
With myriad autovotive fetishes:
Pendulous mascots
Like household gods
In a home from home;
Bumper stickers,
And monogrammed letters and numbers,
Regarded with the same superstition
As the cabbalistic marks
On the forehead of a golem . . .

And America spends 62,000 hours a week
Inside these prosthetic tin cans,
Punched out of cybernetic grease pits,
Then consecrated with creamy white lies.
It seemed to the Visitor that if society wasn't just a rumor,
Cars constituted about seventy per cent of whatever it was.

As a metaphor for society,
They were perfect:
They gave the illusion of freedom
Although they only went on allotted tracks.
They were heavily and uselessly armored.
They fed off repetitive explosions.
You were no one without one.
They were bright, nice, homely, expensive, and hard.
They allowed the sedentary to kill children in a guilt-free fashion,
    much like war.
Their inner workings were years out of date,
And the exclusive prerogative of 'experts' in whose abilities no one
    had any confidence,
Much like bureaucracy.
The heart of a community, the street—
Formerly an intricate web of human interaction—
Was daily torn to shreds:
Dominated, deafened and deadened by the car,
Which had commandeered the idea of progress . . .
Formerly an ideal.

'What happens to General Motors, happens to America':
The Dow-Jones index symbiotically tuned to the state of the automobile;
Each new model frenziedly presented as an economic Holy Grail.
If the new model should fail, society would fall apart.
Each year saw these Great Redeemers of every Northern economy—
Remorselessly produced in car camps by neo-feudal termites under
    militaristic conditions—
Transformed into irredeemable refuse.

It seemed that cars *were* society,
The other thirty per cent an accident. . . .

Lawrence Ferlinghetti

USES OF POETRY

And what is the use of poetry these days
What use is it What good is it
these days and nights in the Age of Autogeddon
in which poetry is what has been paved over
to make a freeway for armies of the night
as in that palm paradiso just north of Nicaragua
where promises made in the plazas
will be betrayed in the back country
or in the so-green fields
of the Concord Naval Weapons Station
where armed trains run over green protesters
where poetry is made important by its absence
the absence of birds in a summer landscape
the lack of love in a bed at midnight
or lack of light at High Noon
in the not-so-White House
For even bad poetry has relevance
for what it does not say
for what it leaves out
Yes what of the sun streaming down
in the meshes of morning
what of white nights and mouths of desire
lips saying Lulu over and over
and all things born with wings that sing
and far far cries upon a beach at nightfall
and light that never was on land and sea
and caverns measured-out by man
where once the sacred rivers ran
near cities by the sea
through which we walk and wander absently
astounded constantly
by the mad spectacle of existence
all these talking animals on wheels
heroes and heroines with a thousand eyes
with bent hearts and hidden oversouls
with no more myths to call their own

(No more myths to live by!
cried Joseph Campbell
and went hull-down in Hawaii)
constantly astounded as I am still
by these bare-face bipeds in clothes
these stand-up tragedians
pale idols in the night streets
trance-dancers in the dust of the Last Waltz
in this time of gridlock Autogeddon
where the voice of the poet still sounds distantly
the voice of the Fourth Person Singular
the voice within the voice of the turtle
the face behind the face of the race
a book of light at night
the very voice of life as Whitman heard it
a wild soft laughter
(ah but to free it still
from the word-processor of the mind!)
And I am a reporter for a newspaper
on another planet
come to file a down-to-earth story
of the What When Where How and Why
of this astounding life down here
and of the strange clowns in control of it
the curious clowns in control of it
with hands upon the windowsills
of dread demonic mills
casting their own dark shadows
into the earth's great shadow
in the end of time unseen
in the supreme hashish of our dream

from

South America Mi Hija

SHARON DOUBIAGO

AMAZON

who wanders grinding frozen syllables
black languages   she comes

with clouds, comes quickly to my veins and my mouth.
She leads us through the streets, her feet
like fine brass, her eyes
like flame of fire

> *"In the beginning God was a couple.*
> *Inkari, a man   Collura, a woman.*
> *Then the Fall.*
> *He said God was a man, the men*
> *we birthed.   And Creation*
> *a war.*
>
> *We waited, having faith, in love with our men,*
> *their children we birthed.*
> *Each time we believed*
> *in our children*
> *God had returned.*
>
> *We loved.*
> *Generation within generation, war*
> *within war, screams within prayers,*
> *his child in my womb, armies*
> *in our labor we waited.*
> *Each love*
> *a new beginning, each birth*
> *a new belief, a new Messiah, a new*
> *Empire*

daughter from mother from grandmother
mother into daughter into granddaughter
son from mother into granddaughter
into great grandson, we waited

generations within civilizations into new races,
our men into cannon fodder, our fathers
into our brothers into our lovers
our husbands making fodder
of their sons, fidelity

into tragedy into absurdity, Penelope
for Ulysses, Kusi Collura
for Ollanta, Son of my Love of my body

into my grandson, *eons*
we waited

for men in their worldmaking
to save us in our race making

for men
to make peace! How much

war, *how much*

flesh, how much suffering, how much hate,
how much history, how much heartbreak,
how much labor, how much

love

how many religions, how many Saviors, how many
nations, how many worlds in ruins, how many
lovers, how many

men

we labored to bring forth
how many men

we held
when they returned

how much they needed, we thought
our femininity, how much we needed
their masculinity, to be part
of their world, how much

strength we gave them as men, how much strength
they gave us as women

but none, though we believed, though we loved,
were made closer
to God

a couple

each woman a new goddess
from which each man
launched

a new war"

SOUTH AMERICA MI HIJA

We Peruvians live in the hope that Inkari will put on his head, his torn arms and legs, and lead us to liberty. That is a legend. But Inkari is Tupaq Amaru and thus the legend is but the signal for the appointed day. From the deepest graves and the most oppressive prisons, from the most subdued people and the most obstinately shackled consciousness, flow legends to make death musical, misery poetic, the darkness of conscience light, forgetfulness loving and loneliness companionable.

Alfonsina Barrionuevo

a. The Shining Path

Walls within walls this Friday night when I walk
into Simon Bolivar's University of Cuzco,
unknown tongues blaring from the speakers
all this first day into the Square of Weeping
when my daughter and I arrive, Marxism, Leninism, Mao Tse-tung,
Sendero Luminoso, Tupaq Amaru.

Stunned, I sit down on the Inca's ancient wall
beneath the porticos that claim it Spanish,
though the moon tells me the stones are alive
and weep. *I have been here before.*
A political convention in French Quebec.
A dream of flight from Vietnam
and a cruel European love
to the California northcoast.

Then I see on my right a great hall of the people assembled
the millions in their native costumes
beneath the great banner that declares
Quechua and Aymara
the first languages of Peru

and I understand as I understand Quechua and Aymara
these people
in the stadium that rises all sides to the ceiling
from the four suyus of the land divided as the seasons
wearing their colors from the planets and stars
their terrible symbols as if from revelations
mask upon mask, flag beyond flag

who rise from their seats roaring *Compadrazgo!*
in whose throats the love and the hate, *tierra o muerte!*
the cries they may die
the knowledge they may have to, the belief
the only way
the path that shines

and I understood as I understand myself
America

b. "*Compadrazgo* means spiritual link between two people"

*In the spring of 1979, Edith Lagos, 15, led a massive high school student
strike in Ayacucho, the first action of Sendero Luminoso. In September
1982, at 19, she was found murdered, cut up by the bayonets of the military
police. Despite intimidation and danger, 30,000 people attended her funeral, almost half the city's population.*

Inside a young woman
so near I still

can touch her, raised
on two stone tiers, wearing
blue jeans, old boots, a fitted
blue velvet jacket

beneath long black
hair. *Inca,* but not
the native costume
of woman. I can

touch her still, she carries on
beneath my stare
as if I'm not here,
lobbying for her right to speak, her
protest. This could be
Berkeley. Boston. It's
Cuzco, female
soul so fierce, intelligent, so
alone, Yma Sumac crying
five octaves around the world
the love and the hate, the strongest
wind, Amerique. She is
any radical girl, so many I have known,
myself, one of three here
in the thirty thousand I watch,
stunned in the high altitude,
having walked
into the real Peru

beautiful men in their pointed knitted hats
with earflaps, red and pink,
their banners and staffs, turquoise and gold,
their purple ponchos, leather sandals, wildest weavings
lobbying for position, their turn
to protest
to cry
comrade! compañero! compadre! compadrazgo!

From what do these people rise?
With what knowledge are they armed?
How do the legends, the music, the poetry, the clothes,
the consciousness
continue to flow, and this girl, Edith
Lagos, mi
hija, mi

virgin

she who belongs to no man's tribe
whose roots she had to cut, more
binding than any man's, more
cutting, more

radical, more
painful

> Inside the woman
> all the people

in whose throat *DESENEADENAR LA FURIA*
DE LA MUJER
now the birds, the cry, the winds
bring the whole hemisphere, Edith Lagos
from the deepest grave, the most
oppressive prison

so near I can touch you still
outside of time, your cheek
of geography, your velvety shoulder, your breasts,
your photo in all my country's papers
where you carry on, *tierra o muerte!* your name
means

battle and *lake,* your blue velvet
over your blue jeans

will be said, will be
sacred, we vow it, Goddess, we
vote it

you are the only revolution
the only future, mi

compadrazga, sweet
girl

> *Edith!*
> *Get up!*
>
> *Put on your head*
> *your torn arms and legs, lead us*

from

Iovis Omnia Plena

ANNE WALDMAN

He catches my eye, my fancy
October
I ride an orange car
The radio is sad & hopeful
"Don't Turn Your Back on Love"
Clouds lift higher
& clutter the mountain
It's in the weather everywhere
I am helpless
Ex Stasis
I'm Gaia
Father Sky look down on me
Stars are his eyes
He enters me
All is full of him

What's true by excluding nothing (I can't really do this): the birthplace, the rain (40 days & 40 nights) observed from a screened porch. Cradle me in memory and make me a goddess-fearing Titan. I didn't resist & pulled my weight, a firecracker to be born in this world. And swept in the tide of this post-war boom, the child of such & such a divine mother and a father, the soul of gentleness. A plain kind of basics weep now to think of modesty in financial matters & hard facts of life, the fanatical enemy war that made sense, the war that hoped to be brought into a safer place, the letters and photographs, you can imagine, & description of dead soldier limbs lifted out of rubble (he saw this, they saw this, they all saw this) the unmitigated trouble of it, and it a mighty cause, and the children everywhere of it now, in my life, of survivors, prisoners, dead ones, tortured or heroic, what could come after this in the nuclear sense? Yet how it "ended," what is the payoff, the result of any way you look at it, those survivors too, the Japanese, and now we live in the combined karma, if I might use that word, dear sister dear Yoshiko, dear reader dear student, in the sense of what continues, a thread of energy perhaps is all. Which is why now I can say the poet must be a warrior of the battlefield of Mars, o give me a break, thank you very much. No one will sign on this dotted sky line. But what is per-

ceived is the vast body, the sky itself, coupled with earth and someone
(Virgil) said: IOVIS OMNIA PLENA. All is full of Jove (his sperm presum-
ably to people Chaos).

>   Whole the moon, whole the year
>   tuliz U   tuliz hab
>   whole the day, whole the night,
>   tuliz kin   tuliz akab
>   whole the breath when it moved too, whole the blood too
>   tuliz ik cu ximbal xan   tuliz kik xan
>   when they came to their beds   their mats, their thrones;
>   tu kuchul tu uayob tu poopoob tu dzamob
>   rhythm in their reading of the good hours,
>   ppiz u caxanticob yutzil kin
>   as they observed the good stars enter their reign,
>   la tu ppiz yilcob yocolob yahaulil utzul ekob tu yahaulil
>   Everything was good
>   Utz tun tulacal

But this is way after the feminine principle is making her mark on universal time equals space. I don't know anything, I know it all. The war is full
of war and Levite laws, not tamed by laws of mercy, and Astoreth goes underground, as women are dragged into caves. And later a cruel Gentile
world. Research: intercourse with mothers & daughters (as beasts do) a
dream:

This was after the fall of the mother earth & giants
I said this already about sweetness
I said My Father, like a small lake
"Creators" as in Greek for poets, yet nothing is created from limitless
mind
but
but this

> The famous artist takes me to a Hotel in a city like Portland. I'm a
> real redhead now, but am concerned about the Dharma test I had to
> take earlier & I have the distinct feeling they'll say I was being too
> literal when I wrote the phrase "Things as they are." I was think-
> ing, then, on the phrase, how I wouldn't have a daughter now that I
> had all these "I"s. Two boy children, where did the second come
> from? Red is now pulling the black slip strap down. I am excited
> but worried about his exotic girlfriend who is brewing Vietnamese
> coffee in the next room. "Wait don't move!" he says as we're about
> to kiss. "Hold that stance!" He pours a bag of cement in the robin's
> egg blue porcelain sink, mixing it with hot water the way you do

henna. Then he picks up a little shovel in front of the fireplace and proceeds to dump the mixture over my head. It feels good and quells desire.

but this desire
is a weekend
a mere idea
I think "50 labels self-sticking"
I think how life is compounded by paper
I think how sleep tonight tomorrow you suffer
I think I'll fall in love with him all over again
Me a Woodswoman from the City of the Mill
Grandfather John a glassblower, sedate in the wind,
spectacled, pale, works hard in the Protestant ethic

Millville, New Jersey which was the epitome of a place small
& human and at the lake the motor boat coming in at dusk.
There was a swing piano style (my father's)
& the chimney he (a father) built on the house never to
be owned ours

LETTER TO MISS IDONA HAND

Millville, Feb 4, 1902

My Darling,

Yours at hand — and I would certainly have been disappointed if I had not received it. I have been resting a little since supper — as I am real tired tonight it is now nearly 7 o'clock and we go to German lessons at 8. I hope you have spent two real nice pleasant days and hope the remainder of the week is or will be just the same and also that you derive lots of good from them. Now my first two days have not been so pleasant I have had some real trials nothing has went well and I feel real out of sorts tonight. I hardly know what I would have done had I not received a letter from someone very precious to me. Well our orders have been running very bad lately. I think things will come better hereafter I hope so anyway. Well this is to much grumbling for you I won't complain any more.

I went out to Church last night. James wanted me to help him sing. Well they had a very good meeting. I think there were two conversions. The young man who they tried to get Sunday night his brother was converted, he was there but would not go but they think he will tonight. May McLaughlin's father was up last night. Mr. Hunter asked that the men invite all of the men in the factory tonight and I think there will be a big time there. Mrs. Hunter is going to sing Memories tonight.

Well I am going to finish up on scolding. Now who said it would do good to be apart awhile I would like to know did I ever say that and mean it? Oh yes! You ought to see my mustache it's a beauty. Well darling feed up well and when you come home Sallie will soon kill the fatted calf. Don't worry about me going skating. No more for me. Remember me to all I will close and go learn a little dutch

> Yours only and truly
>
> John W. Waldman

Admonishing students to avoid writing the grandmother
in the attic, for example, or mother too, think of Creeley &
that respect & ease
To ease the distant dead one
But the mother was hard on the father, dominating 47 MacDougal
Street you must say "below Houston"

A: So talk a little bit about your neighborhood.
R: We're passing the new Golden Pacific National Bank which is kind of a outstanding piece of Chinese architecture, very brand new. And it's already beginning to flake off on the red columns. And they've got outside marble Chinese dragons and we're heading now past the old Centre Street main police station which has been abandoned for ten years, but is about to be opened up as a condominium. And I think it'll be quite a landmark. Now we're, as we get to the corner of Broome and Centre Street, we're looking across to what I believe to be a German-sponsored project which seems also to be some sort of condominium, I . . .
A: . . . are wacky . . . this green . . .
R: Yeah, well that's the old stuff. The building itself has some kind of, it's kind of nice, it looks like . . . I don't know what it looks like, but . . .
A: Yeah, but the windows could be a little. . . ?
R: Yeah, but the new design is, for some reason, somebody chose this kind of aluminum siding . . .
A: Look at that chandelier, I mean, it's so odd . . .
R: Right. And they didn't put anything over their awning there.
A: Germans you said?
R: For some reason, I don't know why, I heard that Germans had taken over the place. Now we're getting up to Cleveland Place and we're passing Eileen's Cheesecake which is a very distinguished product, I certainly sponsor it.
A: Where? Not this.
R: No. We just passed Eileen's. Now we're getting up past the old methadone center, which is now moved up here, which was kind of an outrage in the neighborhood. We're passing Jennifer Bartlett's loft. She was very much against the methadone clinic. Now we're getting even to the

fire station and past PIM magazine, a very cute little miniature gallery, which is also the publisher of probably the smallest publication in New York. And we're heading now past the illustriously renovated Puck Building.

A: And what's the story on the Puck Building?

R: Well, the Puck Building was for years and years like a printed ink building. They manufactured printing ink. And it always smelled very nicely. But since some big entrepreneur has taken it over and done a nice job, it looks pretty glamorous. They've got green trees out here, antibum fences and I think they rent out the ground floor to benefits, big dos, you know. I think Williwear had a do there or something. I don't know who else, but lots of things and probably there's some terrific spaces there. Now right here we're on the corner of Houston and Centre Street or Lafayette Street as it turns, it turns into Lafayette and then turns into Park Avenue, and we're in what I think is filling-station land, where all the cabbies gas up at the gaseteria here, it's an Amoco station on my left. And across the street is the fast parking, gas and wash emporium, which is probably the best place to get your car washed around here. And then there's the attractive Lafayette Tire and Auto Safety Center, sporting a Michelin tire sign and looking pretty jazzy. And there you see the remains of an old City Walls mural. It looks kinda like from Byzantine days. And now we're just passing Houston Street and there's many—Houston Street is still holding about the same pattern with some slight gentrification to the west here, with some new stores on the SoHo side. And now we're heading down, we're heading west on Houston Street, just passing the car wash place. Not much to say about that I haven't already said. Across the street you see the billboard for the Semaphore Gallery which I think is quite interesting, they are changing it every month and doing a nice presentation with a new billboard by the artist they're showing at that, concurrently. That's pretty interesting.

A: That's one of a kind, isn't it?

R: Yeah, I don't know any other gallery that does that. I mean, they, and they only do it at one billboard. And I saw an artist there for the first time that I liked a lot, and then I went to see the show, so it worked on me. Now we're, we just, we're just almost in the heart of SoHo, we're just about to pass, we're passing these new stores. The first of them seems to be called Fuel Injection, which I think is a Japanese, sort of fast-food clothing boutique. And, what's happening, this is the old Lilian Hardware and Supply Co. on the northwest corner. That's been there forever.

Cabbie: Forget about that fifty cents, I hit that by mistake.

R: Right. Thank you. Now, this part of Houston, oh this is a very interesting natural park by I think the artist's name is Sonafest. What's his name, Allen?

A: That sounds right, now you've confused me.

R: Something like that. But it's a very nice experiment to get the landscape exactly back to its natural state. Letting, even letting the weed-like structures come in to play. Now we're passing the Italian, which one is this called?

A: St. Anthony's.

R: Yeah. St. Anthony's. So, I mean, food festival.

A: It's where I grew up. Right here.

R: Thompson Street?

A: Two houses down. The grey house, the red one. I grew up on the top floor.

R: Wow. Doesn't look like it changed much. Are you Italian?

A: No. I wish. No, I'm a Protestant, a Huguenot.

R: And you grew up there?

A: Yeah. I grew up there. My father still lives there.

R: Wow. I didn't know that.

A: My brother's living there now. Forty-seven MacDougal. The St. Anthony's parochial school is across the street, I grew up in the festa and I went to school right on King Street.

R: . . . Canal Street, it's like a forty-dollar number or something.

A: Really. I'll go get one. I have about three at once. They're broken down.

R: Yeah. Go to Canal Street.

A: Which place?

R: It was near, well, they got so many of them. This place happened to be near Centre Street on the north side, very near the corner. On the street, like out at, you know, on a table outside. Now we're into what is really kind of a backwash. I mean, we're near a Martin's bar and I think almost all—

A: (can't hear)   bar.

R: Oh, yeah, the SOB. Actually, I've never been in there, have you?

A: No.

R: Is that like a club, nightclub? Music loft?

A: Yeah. Music loft.

R: But I know this Martin's bar across the way, which is at Varick, and is this Houston?

A: Yeah.

R: Has been there from the year one. And I think almost all Martin's bars were, used to like, be all over the City, or have been torn down or changed.

A: There's a loft for rent.

R: That loft, that loft has been for rent for twenty-five years. I have for years, I have speculated living there for years. Because it's always for rent.

Cabbie: (can't hear)

A: What's that?

Cabbie: They open after-hours places in these lofts now.
A: Open air . . .
R: They're after-hours clubs.
A: Oh, after-hours clubs.

(with Red Grooms)

The cabbie hinted no subject matter but the experience of that father going
to school on the G.I. Bill, studying the beautiful language of literature, &
that was that & could attain right livelihood in such a manner of speaking,
and nailed on the oilcloth to the black table my mother's first husband
built with half Grecian hand upon which we had countless meals and
struggles. And Glaukos surfaced once to defend a poor Mexican, be beaten
up alive still, hospitalized, too gentle in this New York world. Welcome in
this world, Met opera broadcasts and hiding places behind awkward chairs
and fear of oranges from the little brother who came into this world to
make me jealous & wiser. My father on the postwar dream, recovering,
come on get with it, not a Catholic in me, although we are surrounded and
informed and made alive by these visions and rituals & food. I did *too* see
the Devil with the rest of them in the girls' room at P.S. 8! I swear, Mrs.
Mulherne! He was red with horns & a tail & a sneer & he smelled like the
devil too, all spermy & peppery. You could say he was a sex symbol, a voy-
eur (we were so little, pre-pubescent in the long lunchroom hour). The
older half-Greek half-brother confused me with his little black box, Pando-
ra's he called it, a box of woes, the accoutrement of the diabetic. How
many relationships to break a heart? This is for fathers & brothers. A younger golden boy who usurped the breast, the remote father, tamed by war,
the mysterious half-Greek, a dark musician. I honor & obey these first
men in my life who were to repeat in a swirl of patterns & combinations of
other men so dear to me. Should I go on?

President Ronald Reagan
The White House
1600 Pennsylvania Avenue, N.W.
Washington, D.C. 20500

Dear Mr. President:

On November 19 and 20, when you meet with General Secretary
Gorbachev in Geneva, the hopes of not just all Americans, but of the entire
world, will be with you.

Mr. President, I believe that we must take steps to limit the nuclear
arms race.

I recognize that the Soviets are our principal adversaries in the world.
They are tough, determined negotiators. Nevertheless, each of your last
five predecessors—Presidents Kennedy, Johnson, Nixon, Ford, and Carter
—has been able to work out important nuclear arms control treaties with

them—treaties which have helped reduce the threat of nuclear war.

The Geneva summit provides you with a real chance to break the current negotiating impasse—to reach the kind of agreement between leaders which is needed to obtain significant arms control.

As you yourself have said, "A nuclear war cannot be won and must never be fought."

Mr. President, now is the time to put the power of your high office behind those important and telling words. Now is the time to take positive steps to limit the nuclear arms race.

The Geneva summit represents an opportunity to break the arms control stalemate of the last five years and to enact new arms control limits which will <u>strengthen</u>—not weaken—our national security.

I encourage you to seize the opportunity the Geneva summit offers.

Sincerely,

Anne-Who-Grasps-The Broom-Tightly

June 1, 1904

My Dear

I just finished reading your letter and I will say you are rather late in the day to have a bouquet holder made by Saturday. Why tomorrow is Thursday and it would be Sat. before it would come out of the oven. You should have thought of this sooner. You can get one later if you wish. I am very sorry I did not send you the measure for those windows right. But I will get them for you tonight and will mail this letter when I return home. The number on the house is 419. I am very sorry you are having such bad weather but I think it will be clear tomorrow. I understand Mr. Ware to say you told him about the carpet. I will give Mr. Sithers your note tomorrow. Will finish this when I return home tonight. Well it is now 9 o'clock I have been uptown I went out to the house The measure of the windows from centre to bottom of casing is 39 inches. I hardly think the number I told you above is correct It is 417 but I will explain. The double house next to it on the west side is 411 & 413 so I think ours should be 417 but the single house on the east side is 423 There is no number on the house as yet. You have them printed 417. They have 2 rooms papered downstairs—they look real nice Well I will close now hoping that I have everything alright

Ever your John

November 21, 85

Dear Anne,

You tell all and remain mysterious. You've got love to burn. The poem floors me, the words cut me up. Ardent and mute, yes, I am. The dancing does it, but I can't tell, can't speak; I worry, a conscience violated? Afraid of loss, so always losing. Patterns emerge: the legs, a certain shape, the butt, breast, firm, proportion, most important, but aura, it's everything, insepa- rable. The temptation of one who wants more attack.

In La Jolla, the Pacific is Mediterranean blue. The museum's win- dows look out on it, and the art isn't as good. George Trakas, know him? he's renovating a hill there. We dance in the theatre. We flew over you, both ways, and I wanted to stop and ask you how to make life-enhancing love out of this passion-pain.

Your son's becoming a demon perhaps? I and my son, possessed by demons, must become them.

Thanks for the passionate communication. I love you.

> Son: We are lovers & Daddy is a wolf. How old are you Mommy? 44? 29? Mommy you are always 21. Come down to 21 Mommy. Stay 21 forever & I'll grow up to 21. You are not as loud as Dad. You have no scratchy face. You are my most beautiful Mommy.

I get out & am not a sneaking Madam
Not a silhouette
Not a dreamy housekeeper
Not writing the modern Arcadia
Tangibly not at home
The copy on this page, on my shelves, in my heart
  in my room is not a lie
Not mere loneliness, not slipshod
Not metrical, but operating
as pioneer, as trust, as Woman
as Passion, as Champion of Details

My older brother's wife rips up the photograph of his earlier daughter. I struggle in heart with the little godchild my lover commands with him into my world. The male makes us suffer for his heart of hearts. I sleep with my older brother's brother not my blood but who yet resembles him, after sit- ting on my brother's lap in what seems like a long taxi ride (it was raining) home. My mother is trying to keep us apart. We go to Hotel Earle with old man lobby, whore at the door and make illicit love something like incest, unskilled in a burning urge to forge a link. The beautiful god is in town a few days, heading out west. Can I really make love to this yet again another Greek? Too cerebral, unsatisfied. It's the dark connection in this one. I al- ways wore a black turtleneck then. I speak confidently.
The blond on the telephone is a long story, like my younger another broth- er who confesses desire for drugs & men. He takes my virginity as we used to say and we are cheerful in a sullied bed. Because my mother died I can speak these things I state again this is for fathers, brothers, lovers, hus-

bands, son for that is next of kin alive & changing in a fluid world. It is a
palpable motion towards them from one who slumbered many years in the
body of a man and in herself a turf of woman becoming Amazonian in proportions (I grow larger even as I write this) as she spans a continent takes
on the wise mother as she dies. I gave birth to a son to better understand
the men whose messages pour out of me.

Dear Iovis:

Thinking about you: others in you & the way
You are the sprawling male world today
You are also the crisp light in another day
You are the plan which will become clearer with a
    strong border as you are the guest, the student
You are the target
You are the border you are sometimes the map
You are in a car of love
You are never the enemy, dull & flat, dissolving in the sea
Illusion lays its snare, you resort to bait, to tackle me
Our day is gone
To name a place steeped in legend is tempting
To name now & then Nambikwari, Arawak, Poona, makes them appear
We go as far as possible, any old town disappears
We look at the globe from vantage point of sun
The clouds under us are rich with
For manners for trouble for passion we do this to each other
    & forces us back into not-so-terrible childhood
    & forward to old age sickness death you know it
The lines translate to Sanskrit as I say this to you
Exhaustion with phenomena at last
As I say this to you the furniture is rearranged in a sacred text
The room is now long, the room is tall, the room is male
It is a cathedral after you have named them all for me
Or Theodora, a lusty woman
It is All Hallow's Eve & many dead lovers walk tonight
The wind goes through us, we aren't so solid
All you could hold onto I'm knocking out of you
The wind did this when I wasn't looking to me too
Your conscious eyes compel us together
A game of guesses
What is in the gentleman's mind?
Something in you reminds me of a magnate, a planet, a small prayer
A little girl is trapped inside trying to get out of you
I make a new plan every day to ride your mind
Drugs are inconvenient & stand outside the room
In the other room, the "she" carries it off, waving goodbye

The great thing is to love something
the land, the sea, the sweep of a hand, the way something boils
Man is the arm gesture of the woman or something like that says Tim
The battle with the "Ugly Spirit" is not to be discounted says Dan
Andy needed a woman and caressed a tree
Brendan knows maximum intensity is best in this life
A world of heredity quiet in Reed's syllables
A woman's mockery is strong & hearty
She's fond of knowledge learn something about her
The large heart scans the future
Vague unrest I tell you so
You contradict your many selves
Your mind spills out, the page holds on
"You make a man of me" sings radio, gruffly

All is full of Jove, he fucks everything
It is the rough way to prove it
The male gods descend & steal power
How does it happen
How does it happen Blanche Fleur & Heart Sorrow?

Here's how:

I lie back & take him in. He wounds me after a fashion. A new sensation of
art & stimulus, for I watch them both & participate after a fashion until
they are spent & the man is melted in arms, and no longer to do battle on
this bed stage. The bed is the book is the bed is the book where sheets record every muscle tear sweat ooze of life & groan. It is the playground of
the senses for this artist as sweet rehearsal for the nonexistent pages that
will honor this rumbling & panic and lostness. I want to say to dear male
lovers living & dead not anger made this but with due respect in spite of
the crimes of which your sex is prone. I honor the member who is a poten-
tial wand of miracles, who dances for his supper, who is the jester & fool
and sometimes the saint of life. But she, me, who takes it, who responds
clasping with cunt teeth, the receiver, the mountain, whatever it could be
called, the emptying, the joining of this most radiant sphere where the
chakras glow under the sheets or else they are fucking in water, she is witness in this brave act. It feels like the great sperm whale entered me.

The Knock

LAWRENCE FIXEL

> *Kings do not touch doors.*
>
> —Francis Ponge

1

Thinking of what I am about to write, it is already clear how much has changed. That is, having settled into the role of the one whose door is knocked upon (clumsy as that sounds), I have forgotten those times when I stood outside, waiting for someone to respond. Forgotten also those fantasies of the knock as "signal" to the one inside: lover, confederate, secret agent—all actors in the drama of my younger days. . . .

2

Hearing it now, in this present time, I listen for a sound that signifies. Is it a demand or, more moderately phrased, more of an inquiry? Obvious that the light tap, compared to the urgent pounding, sets up a different expectation. Also that each caller has the *choice* of whether to knock or ring the bell. Some constant visitors—as I recall—make the same choice each time; but others, for no apparent reason, alternate between one and the other.

3

The door is our front door, which opens on the street. Those who live at some height, whose doors open onto other doors, must have a different perspective. The image there is of numbered rooms, along a narrow corridor, as in an apartment house or hotel. . . . Does anyone come knocking there? I imagine that the sound is becoming rare. Callers use bell or buzzer; are scrutinized upon a glass screen, or through a slotted opening. . . .

4

The intersection then of a need and a fear. We live in a time, a place, where each encounter is valued or rejected, as it relates to one or to the other. With this in mind, the parameters of "good news," "bad news" can be guessed, seen as predetermined. And if this sounds vague, listen to the voice of another time: *Where I grew up, the doors were always left unlocked.* . . .

5

Memory provides the counterpoint. Leads to another house, another street. To the child who, not long ago, came calling here. As I come to the door, see him standing there, I anticipate the words: *Do you have any cookies!* I open the door wider; he follows me into the kitchen. I reach for the container, lift the lid. . . .

6

The view of the child, of the *as-yet-unrealized*, reminds one of a continuing world, with all its difficulties, dangers. And of a door that can still provide a positive entrance. . . . The knock rather than the bell? It could be that. For however uncertain or peremptory, it proposes a sound unmediated, unchanged by connecting wires. The contact between flesh and wood may also, on some subliminal level, evoke a body as fragile, as endangered as our own.

*

There is a different way to treat this subject. One I would rather not think about, try to remember. It concerns knocking on a wall instead of a door. The sound there would be tentative, holding off desperation. Repeated a second, a third time, there would be more and more urgency. . . . When the response comes—the sound that tells us we are not alone—it would begin again. This time with a careful phrasing; the controlled waiting; and then the slow deciphering of a message we have never heard before.

No Time for Gestures

When we die, we don't leave the world—rather it leaves us.

—Edvard Münch

It has happened so often, that the idea is ingrained. Our journeys have been of limited duration, to a known destination. And each departure has been followed by a return. At some point, however, we start to think about, even prepare for, a departure that is without return. It is then that we find ourselves—like actors learning a new part—rehearsing certain gestures. We wonder then: which is the most appealing, the most appropriate? Lacking an audience, and not trusting the verdict of the mirrors, we can not tell which to choose. We continue setting the scene, summoning various colors and textures, trying to decide about music and speech, makeup and costume. . . . Someone is sure to ask at this point: does it have to be so *theatrical?* We do not respond, but go on arranging the decor, the lights, the shadows. As if we could indeed enhance those last moments with an aura, a special intensity. But the rational mind, breaking in on this complicated reverie, tells us that *this* departure is not what we perform— but what is performed upon us.

*

All this could be written by anyone—with just an adequate imagination— in touch with their deepest fears and longings. What can not be written, planned for, is what happens to come our way. As for instance this letter from a friend who quotes these words of Edvard Münch. Now it has come to my attention, I have still to think more and longer of what it means. If I read it right, there is no time for gestures. For it is not departure that we face, but an abrupt, unprecedented abandonment. . . .

WHO'S WHO IN THE REVIEW

VYT BAKAITIS is a New York-based poet whose *City Country* is forthcoming from Fatal Skin Editions.

VOLKER BRAUN, born in Dresden in 1939, is a printer, machinist, construction laborer, poet, philosopher, playwright and dramaturgist with the famous Berliner Ensemble.

LUCIA BERLIN is a creator of fine short fiction. *Safe & Sound*, a new collection of stories, will soon see the light courtesy of Poltroon Press.

LISA BERNSTEIN edits the *Five Fingers Review*. *The Transparent Body*, a book of her poetry, will appear in 1989 in Wesleyan University Press' New Poets Series.

JAMES BROOK, San Francisco poet, has translated works by Benjamin Péret, Gellu Naum, Alberto Savinio, and Victor Serge.

FERDINANDO CAMON won Italy's 1986 Strega Prize. His novels *Life Everlasting* and *The Fifth Estate* have been published in English by the Marlboro Press.

ALEXANDER COCKBURN'S *Corruptions of Empire* was recently published by Verso. He is an often-embattled political commentator and a regular contributor to *The Nation*, the *LA Weekly*, and *The Atlantic Monthly*.

MARK COOVELIS is the author of *Love Is Something Else: Stories*, which won the James D. Phelan Award in 1987 and the Mary Roberts Rinehardt Award for a first book of fiction in 1988.

LESLIE DICK is a young American expatriate writer living in the U.K., whose formidable first novel, *Without Falling*, is about to fall on the U.S. as a City Lights Book.

DIANE DI PRIMA'S underground *Memoirs of a Beatnik* has resurfaced in a Paragon Press edition. A new poetry collection to be published by City Lights Books in 1989 spans the early beat period to recent feminist, Buddhist-alchemical work.

SHARON DOUBIAGO'S most recent visions are embodied in *The Book of Seeing with One's Own Eyes* (Graywolf Press).

CLAYTON ESHLEMAN edits the sometimes incendiary quarterly *Sulfur*. *The Name Encanyoned River* was recently given wings by Black Sparrow Press.

LAWRENCE FERLINGHETTI has just published a novel set in France during the May events of '68: *Love in the Days of Rage* (Dutton).

LAWRENCE FIXEL'S *Glimmers*, a collection of aphorisms, is his most recent show of light.

TODD GITLIN is Associate Professor of Sociology at University of California, Berkeley. His latest books are: *The Sixties: Years of Hope, Days of Rage* and *Inside Prime Time*.

ROLAND GRYBAUSKAS is the author of a book of poetry called *Desperado of Love*.

MARILYN HACKER, who has won a National Book Award for Poetry, is the author of *Love, Death, and the Changing of the Seasons*.

SEAN A. HIGGINS' translations from the Spanish have appeared in *Index On Censorship*.

CHRISTOPHER HITCHENS is an incisive critic and political chronicler, writing in *The Nation*, *The Spectator* and *The Times Literary Supplement*.

ANSELM HOLLO'S most recent book is *Pickup The House* (Coffee House Press).

LA LOCA is a southern California performance poet destined for fame and agape.

FEDERICO GARCIA LORCA'S two books *Poem of the Deep Song* and *Ode to Walt Whitman & Other Poems* were published by City Lights in 1988.

GIORGIO MANGANELLI is an Italian novelist, critic and playwright, once part of the avant-garde "Group 63." His *Centuria* was awarded the Viareggio Prize.

BERNADETTE MAYER lives and breathes in New York City. Her latest book is *Utopia* (United Artists Books).

JONAS MEKAS, born in Lithuania in 1922, is a major innovator in the independent American cinema.

ANTHONY MOLINO is a psychoanalyst-in-training in Philadelphia. He has translated works by Antonio Porta, Ferdinando Camon, and Valerio Magrelli.

JAMES PURDY'S classic novel *In a Shallow Grave* has just been unearthed and resurrected by City Lights Books.

CRISTINA PERI ROSSI, born in Uruguay in 1941 and living in exile in Barcelona, has published eight collections of short fiction, two novels and six books of poetry.

JOHN SATRIANO has translated Ennio Flaiano's *The Loneliness of the Satyr* and a book of essays by Alberto Moravia.

EDWARD W. SAID is Parr Professor of English and Comparative Literature at Columbia University. His books include *The Question of Palestine* and *Orientalism*.

ROY SCHNEIDER lives in San Diego. His first book, *I know What You Look Like Naked* received excited critical acclaim.

RICHARD SILBERG is Associate Editor of *Poetry Flash* and the creator of *Translucent Gears* (North Atlantic Books).

MELODY SUMNER of Burning Books is the author of a book of short stories, *The Time Is Now*. She also creates music, spoken-word tapes, and radio shows.

WILL STAPLE works as a poet in Nevada City and Grass Valley Schools, and has spent the last 25 Easters in the Grand Canyon. His books are *Passes For Human* and *Coyote Run*.

CHRISTOPHER SAWYER-LAUÇANNO is the author of *The Destruction of the Jaguar; Poems From the Books of Chilam Balam* (City Lights) and *An Invisible Spectator; a Biography of Paul Bowles*, to be published next year by Weidenfeld & Nicolson.

JAYNE LYN STAHL'S poems have appeared in *Exquisite Corpse, Beatitude,* and *New York Quarterly*. Living in L.A., she tries hard to find angels in concrete.

JANINE POMMY VEGA lives in Bearsville, New York, and is the cofounder and director of the Sing Sing Poetry Workshop. Just out is her anthology of prison poetry: *Candles Burn In Memory Town* (Segue).

HEATHCOATE WILLIAMS is the peripatetic British author of the legendary plays *AC/DC* and *The Local Stigmatic*.

ANNE WALDMAN is codirector of the poetry program at Naropa Institute in Boulder, Colorado. Her selected poems will be published in 1989 by Coffee House Press.

TOSHIRO YAMAZAKI, born in Chiba, Japan, in 1960, is studying English language poetry at New College of California.

AIDS Forum Contributors:

KATHY ACKER: Latest ingenious work of fiction: *Empire of the Senseless*.

ROBERTA ALLEN: Visual artist; *The Traveling Woman* is her book of illustrated short stories.

SAM AMBLER has read *After the Howl* at the Berkeley Repertory Theater and Stanford University (as part of their AIDS Commemoration Week).

LYNDA BARRY: Her art and coloring books include *Girls and Boys*, and *Naked Ladies Naked Ladies Naked Ladies*.

DARA BIRNBAUM: Internationally renowned video artist; 1987 recipient of American Film Institute's Maya Deren Award for Independent Film and Video Makers.

JAMES BROUGHTON: Filmmaker, poet, and author of *Seeing the Light* and other illuminating works.

SUE COE: Creator of spectacular political paintings and books: *How to Commit Suicide in South Africa*, *Police State*, and *X*.

JACK COLLINS: Poet-novelist-essayist teaching Gay & Lesbian Studies at City College, San Francisco.

KAREN FINLEY: *The Constant State of Desire* is a recent breathtaking performance piece, now included on the LP *The Truth is Hard to Swallow*.

ROBERT GLÜCK: San Francisco writer: *Jack the Modernist*, *Andy*, and *Elements of a Coffee Service*.

LEON GOLUB: Renowned Chicago painter: his works included in Whitney Biennial.

ABBIE HOFFMAN: Latest blast: *Steal This Urine Test: Fighting Drug Hysteria in America*.

GARY INDIANA: His critical writing and fiction has surfaced in *Artforum*, *Art in America*, *Bomb*, *Between C & D*; a forthcoming novel is called *Horse Crazy*.

GREGORY KOLOVAKOS: Translator of Latin American literature, fiction writer, and Director of the Literature Program of the New York State Council on the Arts.

CAROL LEIGH: *Pope Don't Preach (I'm Terminating My Pregnancy)* is a recent video; she is a contributor to *Sex Work: Writings by Women in the Sex Industry*.

DUANE MICHALS: His recent books *The Nature of Desire* and *Sleep and Dreams* offer haunting photographic sequences.

COOKIE MUELLER: Fiction writer and actress, writing a regular column in *Details* magazine; author of *How to Get Rid of Pimples*.

EILEEN MYLES: New York City poet who has given us *Bread & Water*, and *Sappho's Boat*.

CINDY PATTON: Former editor of *Gay Community News*; author of *Sex and Germs: the Politics of AIDS*. (Watch for groundbreaking article in Fall issue of *Outlook*.)

RACHEL ROSENTHAL: Artist whose subjects are death (*The Death Show*), animal rights (*The Others*, *TRAPS*), nuclear disaster (*Was Black*), fear of pain (*Taboo Subjects*).

SARAH SCHULMAN: Writer of fiction and mysteries. *People in Trouble*, to be published in 1989, is about AIDS activism.

CHARLES SEXTON: Bay Area painter now completing his MFA at the San Francisco Art Institute.

NANCY SPERO: Visual artist whose works have been exhibited in galleries worldwide.

LYNNE TILLMAN: Writer and filmmaker; contributor to *Bomb* and *Between C & D*; author of *Haunted Houses* and *Home Sick*.

EDMUND WHITE: Author of great American novels; his latest work is *The Darker Proof: Stories from a Crisis*, with Adam Mars-Jones.

DAVID WOJNAROWICZ: His artworks shown at the Whitney Biennial; out of the ring next year is his new book: *Self-Portrait in 23 Rounds; A Psychic Walkabout*.

CITY LIGHTS PUBLICATIONS

Angulo de, Jaime and Gui. JAIME IN TAOS
Antler. FACTORY
Artaud, Antonin. ARTAUD ANTHOLOGY
Bataille, Georges. THE TEARS OF EROS
Bataille, Georges. EROTISM: Death and Sensuality
Bataille, Georges. STORY OF THE EYE
Baudelaire, Charles. TWENTY PROSE POEMS
Baudelaire, Charles. INTIMATE JOURNALS
Bowles, Paul. A HUNDRED CAMELS IN THE COURTYARD
Breá, Juan. RED SPANISH NOTEBOOK
Brecht, Stefan. POEMS
Broughton, James. SEEING THE LIGHT
Buckley, Lord. HIPARAMA OF THE CLASSICS
Buhle, Paul, ed. FREE SPIRITS
Bukowski, Charles. THE MOST BEAUTIFUL WOMAN IN TOWN
Bukowski, Charles. TALES OF ORDINARY MADNESS
Bukowski, Charles. NOTES OF A DIRTY OLD MAN
Burroughs, William S. THE BURROUGHS FILE
Burroughs, William S. THE YAGE LETTERS
Cardenal, Ernesto. FROM NICARAGUA, WITH LOVE
Carrington, Leonora. THE HEARING TRUMPET
Cassady, Neal. THE FIRST THIRD
Choukri, Mohamed. FOR BREAD ALONE
CITY LIGHTS REVIEW #1
CITY LIGHTS REVIEW #2
Codrescu, Andrei, ed. EXQUISITE CORPSE READER
Comford, Adam. ANIMATIONS
Corso, Gregory. GASOLINE
David-Neel, Alexandra. SECRET ORAL TEACHINGS IN
    TIBETAN BUDDHIST SECTS
Deleuze, Gilles. SPINOZA:PRACTICAL PHILOSOPHY
Dick, Leslie. WITHOUT FALLING
DiPrima, Diane. REVOLUTIONARY LETTERS
Doolittle, Hilda (H.D.) NOTES ON THOUGHT & VISION
Ducornet, Rikki. ENTERING FIRE
Duras, Marguerite. DURAS BY DURAS
Eberhardt, Isabelle. THE OBLIVION SEEKERS
Fenollosa, Ernest. THE CHINESE WRITTEN
    CHARACTER AS A MEDIUM FOR POETRY
Ferlinghetti, Lawrence. LEAVES OF LIFE
Ferlinghetti, Lawrence. PICTURES OF THE GONE WORLD
Ferlinghetti, Lawrence. SEVEN DAYS IN NICARAGUA LIBRE
García Lorca, Federico. ODE TO WALT WHITMAN &
    OTHER POEMS
García Lorca, Federico. POEM OF THE DEEP SONG
Gascoyne, David. A SHORT SURVEY OF SURREALISM
Ginsberg, Allen. HOWL & OTHER POEMS
Ginsberg, Allen. KADDISH & OTHER PEOMS
Ginsberg, Allen. REALITY SANDWICHES
Ginsberg, Allen. PLANET NEWS
Ginsberg, Allen.THE FALL OF AMERICA
Ginsberg, Allen. MIND BREATHS
Ginsberg, Allen. PLUTONIAN ODE
Ginsberg, Allen. IRON HORSE
Ginsberg, Allen. INDIAN JOURNALS
Ginsberg, Allen. SCENES ALONG THE ROAD

Connexions is **THRILLED**

about international perspectives!

Connexions presents the experiences and struggles of women abroad in their own words and in their own voices. Each issue focuses on a specific theme. Find out what women all over the world have to say about Health, Sexuality, Migration, and Girls Growing Up... **SUBSCRIBE** to *Connexions, An International Women's Quarterly* **NOW!**

☐ **I would like to subscribe!**
  ☐ One year, $12
  ☐ Libraries and Institutions, $24
  ☐ Canada and Mexico, US$14
  ☐ Overseas Airmail, US$20, Surface US$14

☐ I would like more information about
Connexions, An International Women's Quarterly

Name_____

Address_____

City, St.,ZIP_____

Make US checks or international money orders or travelers checks payable to People's Translation Service and mail to Connexions, 4228 Telegraph Ave., Oakland CA 94609

YOU'RE NOT GETTING ALONG WITHOUT IT

"The best urgent literary reading in the country."

Andrei Codrescu, *Baltimore Sun*

• • • • • • •

36 PAGE TRIANNUAL ESTABLISHED 1981, EDITED AND PUBLISHED BY JENNIFER DUNBAR DORN, PETER MICHELSON, EDWARD DORN AND SIDNEY GOLDFARB.

• • • • • • •

3 ISSUES $7.50, $10 INSTITUTIONS, $14 OUTSIDE U.S. AND CANADA.   AVAILABLE BACK ISSUES $4.00.

IF IT MOVES PRINT IT

ROLLING STOCK
CAMPUS BOX 226, UNIVERSITY OF COLORADO, BOULDER 80309.

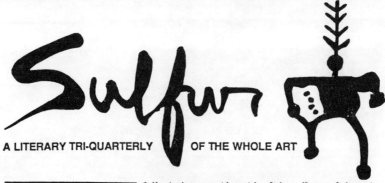

Sulfur

A LITERARY TRI-QUARTERLY **OF THE WHOLE ART**

Editor
Clayton Eshleman

NCR Editor
Jed Rasula

Contributing Editors
Rachel Blau DuPlessis
Michael Palmer
Eliot Weinberger
John Yau

Correspondents
Charles Bernstein
James Clifford
Clark Coolidge
Marjorie Perloff
Jerome Rothenberg

Managing Editor
Caryl Eshleman

Sulfur is Antaeus with a risk. It has efficacy. It has primacy. It is one of the few magazines that is more than a receptacle of talent, actually contributing to the shape of present day literary engagement.

— George Butterick

Sulfur must certainly be the most important literary magazine which has explored and extended the boundaries of poetry. Eshleman has a nose for smelling out what was going to happen next in the ceaseless evolution of the living art.

— James Laughlin

In an era of literary conservatism and sectarianism, the broad commitment of *Sulfur* to both literary excellence and a broad interdisciplinary, unbought humanistic engagement with the art of poetry has been invaluable. Its critical articles have been the sharpest going over the last several years.

— Gary Snyder

Founded at the California Institute of Technology in 1981, Sulfur magazine is now based at Eastern Michigan University. It appears 3 times a year, averages 200 pages per issue, and includes poetry by established post World War II poets (Olson, Duncan, Ginsberg) as well as younger writers, archival materials (Pound, Williams, Crane), translations (Artaud, Césaire, Paz), artwork (Golub, Petlin, Kitaj), and a 60 page section per issue of notes, correspondence and book reviews.

NAME_____

ADDRESS _____

CITY_____ STATE _____ ZIP_____

☐ $15 for 3 issues (individuals)

☐ $22 for 3 issues (institutions)

Start with ☐ the most recent issue ☐ issue #___

Mail check to SULFUR, English Department, Eastern Michigan Univ., Ypsilanti, MI 48197
For information: 313 / 483-9787

CALIBAN

Caliban is redefining the avant-garde.

Issue Number 3:
The New Modern • Interviews with Porta and Stone
Kelly • Berssenbrugge • McGrath • Kauffman • McClure
Mori • Stoloff • Hitchcock • Martinez • Balestrini • Hess
Gallagher • Schmitz • Comolli • Anderson • Curbelo
Lincoln • Komunyakaa • Malanga • Carruth • Peterson
Bly • Crevel by Rattray • Chédid by Roditi

Subscriptions: Individuals—$8/one year, $15/two years
Institutions—$15 per year; Issues 1, 2 and 3—$5 each

CALIBAN, Lawrence R. Smith, Editor
P.O. Box 4321, Ann Arbor, MI 48106

Edward Said on Kipling
Lincoln Kirstein, an autobiography
Eve Kosofsky Sedgwick, the epistemology of the closet
Elaine Showalter on male feminism
John Hollander, poems and essays
Harold Bloom on the epic hero
C.L.R. James on cricket in the West Indies

RARITAN

A Quarterly Review edited by Richard Poirier

Cutting across intellectual disciplines
and exploring the boundaries of new ones

Subscriptions: ☐ $16/one year   ☐ $26/two years
Make checks payable to RARITAN, 165 College Ave., New Brunswick, NJ 08903
Sorry, we cannot bill.

Name

Address

City, State, Zip

Subscribe now and receive a free copy of
The Selected Letters of William James
edited and introduction by Elizabeth Hardwick

ACM ACM ACM ACM ACM

ANOTHER CHICAGO MAGAZINE *ACM*

ACM *ACM*

"Consistently exciting and valuable."
San Francisco Review of Books

"Beautifully designed and
clearly edited…a stimulating
blend of poetry, fiction,
photographs, cartoons, and
reviews…Recommended."
Choice Magazine

Ask for ACM at your local bookstore or send us
$5.00 for a sample copy and we'll pay the postage.
Distributed to the trade by Ingram Periodicals,
Bookslinger, Cornucopia. Another Chicago Press,
Box 11223, Chicago, IL 60611.

**Democracy, education and social progress
depend on the printed word.**

**U.S./NICA
PRINTERS PROJECT**
COMMITTED TO KEEPING THE PRESSES
ROLLING IN THE NEW NICARAGUA

Nicaragua's printing and typesetting equipment is breaking down.
They need our help to keep it running.

For more information, contact:

U.S./NICA Printers Project
Box 282, 3309½ Mission Street, San Francisco, CA 94110 (415) 285-8548
Sponsored by TecNica and the Institute for Technology and Development.

RED BASS #13

Kathy Acker, Carolee Schneemann, James
Purdy, Nancy Spero, Charles Gatewood,
Johanna Went, Elizam Escobar, Joseph
Nechvatal, Paul Laraque, Ivan Arguelles,
Claude Pelieu, Lynne Augeri, Peter Plate

$ 5 sample copy
$10 subscription
$15 institutions
$15 foreign

RED BASS • **2425 Burgundy St.** • **New Orleans, LA 70117**

TriQuarterly

Fiction • Poetry • Art • Criticism
Three times a year

The New York Times has called **TriQuarterly** "perhaps the pre-eminent journal for literary fiction" in the nation. **Chicago** magazine describes it as "one of the best, issue after issue." But see for yourself—subscribe now . . .

Recent and forthcoming contributors:

Grace Paley
Nadine Gordimer
Thomas McGrath
C. K. Williams
Reynolds Price
Carol Bly
Stuart Dybek
Robert Boswell
Gloria Emerson
Irina Ratushinskaya
Michael S. Harper

Derek Walcott
William Goyen
Robert Stone
Donald Davie
Linda Pastan
Maxine Kumin
Tobias Wolff
E. P. Thompson
Cyrus Colter
Mary Lee Settle
. . . and many new voices

TriQuarterly Northwestern University 2020 Ridge Avenue Evanston, IL 60208
SUBSCRIBE!

☐ 1 year ($18) ☐ 2 years ($32) ☐ life ($150)

Please enter my subscription

☐ I enclose $_____   ☐ Please bill me

☐ Charge my VISA/Master Card # _____

Signature _____ Exp. date _____

Name _____

Address _____

City _____ State _____ Zip _____

CITY LIGHTS

A Literary Meetingplace Since 1953

Bookselling & Publishing in the great tradition
of independent international bookstores

261 Columbus Avenue (at Kerouac Alley)
San Francisco California 94133
[415] 362-8193 Booksellers   [415] 362-1901 Publishers
Please write for our mail order catalog